FIRST AID FOR DOGS

FIRST AID FOR DOGS

by George E. Boyle, V.M.D.
and Charles L. Blood

DEMBNER BOOKS·NEW YORK

Dembner Books

Published by Red Dembner Enterprises Corp., 80 Eighth Avenue, New York, N.Y. 10011
Distributed by W. W. Norton & Company, Inc., 500 Fifth Avenue, New York, N.Y. 10110

Library of Congress Cataloging-in-Publication Data

Boyle, George E.
  First aid for dogs.

  Includes index.
  1. Dogs—Wounds and injuries—Treatment. 2. Dogs—
Diseases—Treatment. 3. First aid for animals.
I. Blood, Charles E. II. Title.
SF991.B69 1988 636.7'08960252 88-6999
ISBN 0-942637-03-8 (pbk.)

CONTENTS

A SUGGESTION FOR USING THIS BOOK

Two forms of first aid are presented here. One describes procedures to be applied to specific injuries. The other is preventive in nature, to ensure that emergencies are less likely to arise.

The authors recommend that you read the book completely, then keep it readily available as a reference. Knowing beforehand what measures can and should be taken to cope with an emergency will save you precious time just when time is needed most.

The procedures described or demonstrated in this book are widely recognized as those for use in general first aid. Each case, however, can present specific complications. Therefore, it is imperative in all cases that you contact your veterinarian as soon as possible.

1 TICKS AND LARGER SKIN PROBLEMS

The condition of your hair and skin reflects how you maintain your health and what you eat. The same is true of your dog.

The signs a dog has a skin problem are obvious. They include loss of hair, redness, excessive chewing and scratching. Whether the cause of the problem is parasitic, glandular, bacterial, or fungal in nature must be determined by veterinary diagnostic means.

Basically, the care of your dog's skin and coat is a matter of common sense. Most important is common sense in diet.

Don't give your dog vitamin supplements or extra anything unless your veterinarian says the animal needs it. A working dog—a sheepdog for example—might require additional protein in its diet while a lap dog wouldn't.

Don't attempt to formulate your dog's diet yourself. There's as much research into dog food these days as there is into people food. Most commercial dog foods supply a fully balanced diet. They satisfy all the average dog's nutritional needs and do it better than you could if you undertook to prepare the food yourself.

Never forget that a healthy skin and coat go from the inside out. What you do on the outside is an afterthought, but even some afterthoughts deserve consideration. Here are some practices to follow in caring for your dog's coat.

1. In winter, when the heat is on in your house, the animal's coat may tend to dry out. Dietary coat supplements can correct this problem. Consult your veterinarian.

2. Applying creams and ointments to cure dry or inflamed skin will ease the condition temporarily—but only temporarily. If the condition persists, see your veterinarian.

3. A good brushing gets rid of dead hair and dead skin, and stimulates circulation.

4. When washing a healthy skin and coat, don't use herbal or deodorant soap or anything even close to a harsh detergent. Use baby shampoo or

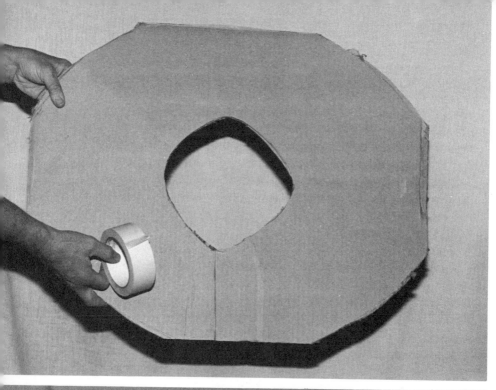

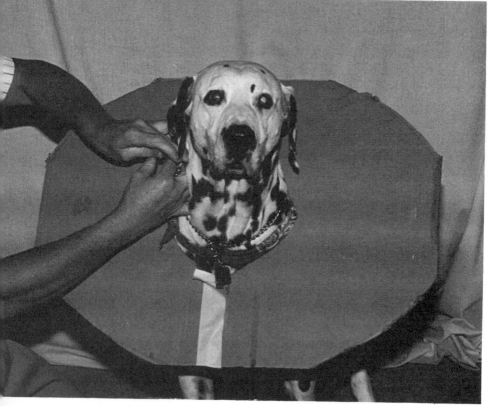

Elizabethan collar. Cut a piece of cardboard as shown. Make sure the center hole will fit comfortably around your dog's neck and that the collar is wide enough to prevent the animal from reaching around it with its teeth. About twice as wide as the dog is from shoulder to shoulder is a good, general rule. Slit the collar at the bottom, slip it over the dog's head and tape the slit closed.

glycerine soap. Then rinse, rinse, and rinse again. Even the mildest cleaners can cause irritation if left on the skin.

The Elizabethan Collar. It looks horrible, but without it, any first aid measures you take for a skin injury will be quite promptly undone by your dog's tongue or teeth. The undoing only makes things worse.

The collar is not cruel. The animal is totally mobile, quickly learns to eat and drink while wearing it, experiences no choking, and is otherwise able to function normally. He or she simply can't get at that itch or irritation "back there" and, being a dog and stoic in nature, soon decides to put up with it.

SPECIFIC INJURIES

Minor scrapes. A scrape is only minor if the skin hasn't been broken. Nothing more than loss of hair and a raw spot is the result. The injury seldom requires a veterinarian's care.

Gently wash the area with a mild solution of bland soap and water—or just clean water. Apply plain pertroleum jelly, such as Vaseline, or a first aid cream containing an antibiotic two or three times a day until redness, sensitivity, and swelling are gone.

Don't worry about that bald spot. The hair will grow in nicely in four to six weeks.

Minor lacerations/punctures. Here the skin is broken and open to infection. There is some bleeding—not serious—and the wound probably doesn't require stitches.

If all the above are true, you can treat the injury at home. (Unless you think the injury was caused by another animal, in which case, see 'Animals Bites,' page 12, and ignore everything that follows here except applying direct pressure to the bleeding and transporting the animal to your veterinarian.)

Let the wound bleed for a short time to cleanse itself before applying pressure directly to the spot. After you're certain the bleeding has stopped, use a good pair of scissors to close-clip the hair around the wound.

Clipping hair in cases of lacerations or punctures. Using a soft pad or sponge, wash the area to be clipped with a mild soap and water solution. Pat dry. For the actual clipping, we recommend a curved pair of scissors, basically a large version of cuticle scissors. They're available at most pharmacies. Clip the area close and clean as shown.

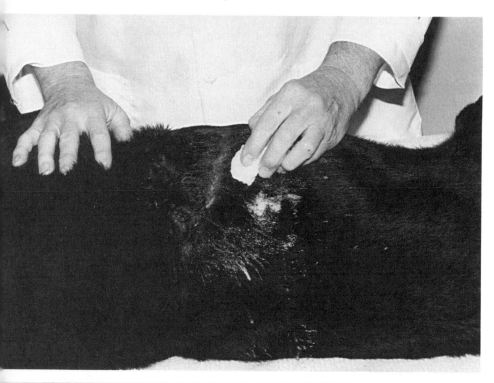

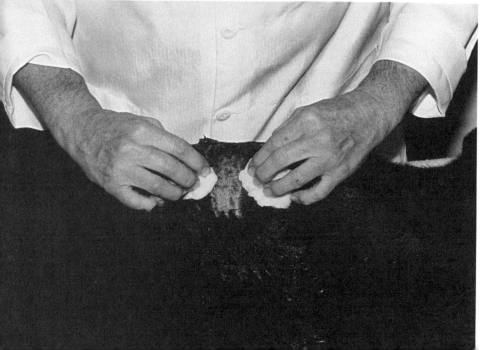

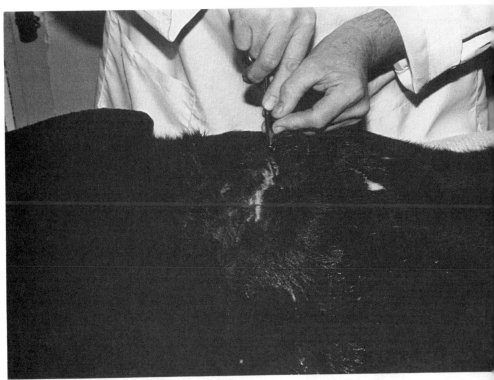

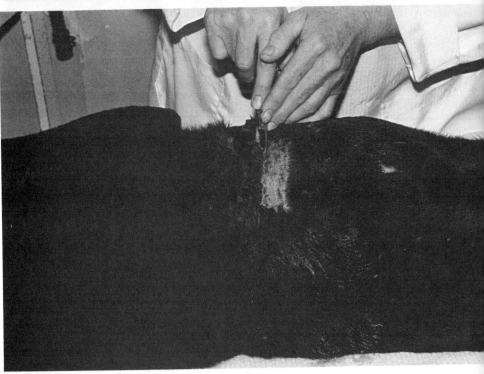

After flushing the clipped area generously with clean water, carefully spread the wound open with your fingertips. There's little, if any, pain caused by what you do next, so don't be squeamish about it.

Applying medication to lacerations or punctures. Dip a cotton swab in plain petroleum jelly or a mild first aid cream and apply it to the inside of the wound. To do this, you have to spread the edges of the wound with your fingers. We're demonstrating how with a human model in the interest of clarity.

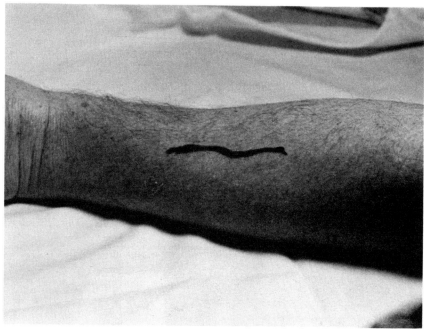

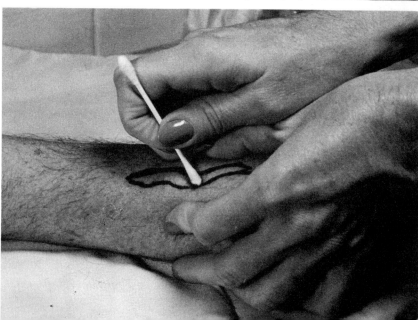

Caution: If, after twenty-four to forty-eight hours, the injury becomes hot, reddened, or sensitive, an infection is going on in there. Take your dog to your veterinarian immediately.

Deep lacerations. Damage to the skin is severe. Muscle tissue is torn, and there is moderate to heavy bleeding.

Don't try to figure out whether the bleeding is arterial or otherwise. Wet down a clean gauze pad or T-shirt and apply direct pressure immediately. When the bleeding is under control, flush the area with clean water, apply a pressure bandage as shown, and transport the animal to the veterinarian or clinic.

If it's going to be a while before you can get to your doctor, giving your dog an aspirin or two, as described in Chapter 12, page 91, may help calm it and make everything easier on both of you.

Pressure bandages for deep lacerations. Fold a clean, lint-free cloth pad to cover the wound and firmly hold it against the injury. Maintain the pressure while you secure the pad in place with gauze bandage.

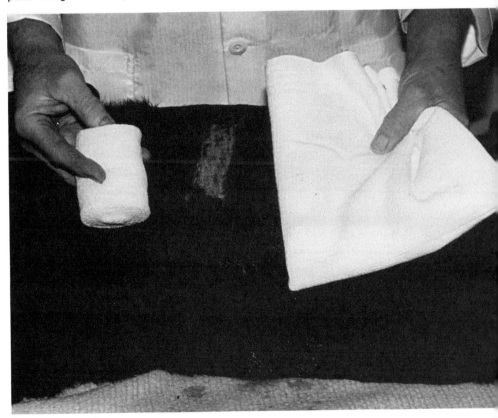

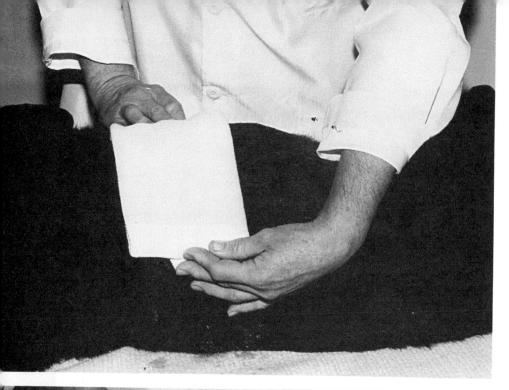

Minor burns (scalding). This most common of burns occurs, as you'd expect, in the kitchen. Such accidents are instantly followed by the scalded dog's owner going in one direction and the scalded dog in the other.

You can't expect the dog to do anything but run away from the thing that burned it. The responsibility to keep calm is solely yours.

To keep the burn from getting worse, cool it down. Immediately. It may be difficult and even risky to handle the animal—it is both hurt and angry—so you may have to muzzle it or restrain it, as shown in Chapter 10, pages 78–79, or at least get some help. Once you've accomplished either or both, douse the burned area repeatedly with cold water. By the bucketful, in the kitchen sink, the bathtub, or with a garden hose. Pour it on.

This not only cools off the burned area, it reduces the chance of deeper damage. If the skin ia allowed to "cook"—which is exactly what happens if you don't cool it down—the injury could become more serious.

If the scald covers a large area, transport your dog to the veterinarian immediately.

If the scalded area is small—remember a burn on your dog looks just like a burn on you—you can treat it yourself.

Clip the area around the burn as thoroughly as possible with scissors. Then—using soap, not shaving cream—carefully shave the whole area until you've cleared a space an inch or two beyond the burn itself. Next, apply any first aid cream, preferably one containing an antibiotic and cortisone, or any hand cream, ointment, or lotion containing aloe. If you have nothing else, us plain petroleum jelly.

Minor burns (chemical). The things you depend on to keep your bathroom spotless and floors clean can and will burn your dog. So can the shampoo you use to rid your dog of fleas—if you don't thoroughly rinse it off.

Treat a minor chemical burn as you would a scald. Drown it with water, shave the area, and apply the same kind of cream, lotion, or ointment you'd use for scalds. However, if the burn is caused by a strong chemical—drain cleaner, for example—read the manufacturer's recommendations on the container's label. They may call for your adding vinegar or baking soda to the water.

Turpentine burns. This oily liquid can cause severe burning and systemic reactions.

You don't have to be told oil and water do not mix, so never reach for the cold water as you would for heat or chemical burns. Instead, reach immediately for a bottle of mineral oil. Not mineral spirits—*mineral oil*.

Rub it in thoroughly and generously to absorb the turpentine. Then, as thoroughly, wash your dog with baby shampoo. Afterward, treat the inflamed skin as you would a minor burn.

Never try to remove paint from your dog with turpentine. Use mineral oil to loosen the paint, then wash it off.

Frostbite. It's a superficial, minor burn, so let's talk about it.

Frostbite occurs mostly in the extremities. The paws, ears, and scrotum are most frequently affected. The latter is often the result of sitting in a snowbank too long.

The trouble with frostbite is you don't usually know your dog has been "bitten" until the next day, when the area becomes swollen and uncomfortable, and the animal begins to fuss. So, when your dog comes in from the cold and shows any sign of discomfort, such as licking at its paws, take it immediately into a warm room, wrap with a large towel—or a small, light blanket if it's too big for a towel—and gently massage the frostbitten area to stimulate circulation.

If you miss the warning signs, and irritation sets in, treat the frostbite by gently applying any of the ointments, creams, or lotions previously mentioned for the treatment of scalds and chemical burns.

Electric burns. It will probably only try this once, but a puppy teething on a lamp cord can suffer secondary burns to the mouth.

If the burns are not severe, wash the mouth out with cold water and rub in—don't merely apply—a bland first aid cream.

Electric burns. Don't dab and don't be shy. Put a generous amount of first aid cream on your fingertip, hold the dog's lips aside and make sure the cream is gently but thoroughly massaged into and around the burned area.

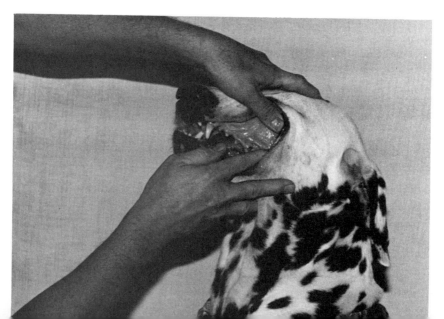

Warning: An electrical burn can be a great deal worse than it first appears to be. Some very severe burns are not always visible, but the internal damage they cause may result in death three or four days later. The rule to follow is this: If your dog receives a shock, take it to your veterinarian immediately.

Severe burns. With such burns, the dog's first line of defense, its skin, has been lost. The animal may go into shock, and there is real danger of fluid loss.

Do not douse your dog with water as you would with a minor burn. *Do not try to treat the burned area.* Keep the animal warm and its breathing passages open until it is obviously not in shock, but is alert and anxious about its condition.

The battle here is against dehydration. Try to coax your dog to drink a solution of one-half teaspoon of salt and one-half teaspoon of sodium bicarbonate (baking soda) in a quart of water. If the animal can't be coaxed, you must force fluids into it. Soon and frequently.

Get the injured dog to your veterinarian as fast as possible. If you are going to be delayed, treat the burned—in this case, charred—area yourself.

Forcing fluids for severe burns. There's a nice, big pocket between teeth and lips at the rear of your dog's mouth. Hold it open while you hold the animal's jaws closed. Use a paper or plastic cup to literally pour the salt or sodium bicarbonate and water solution down its throat. Pour gently, though, to avoid choking or gagging.

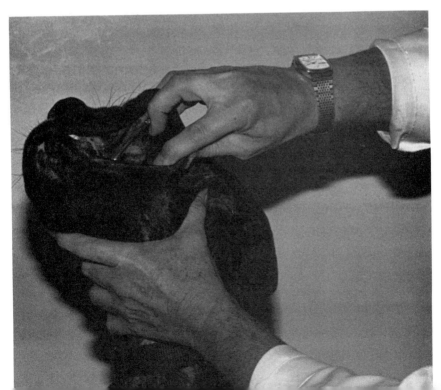

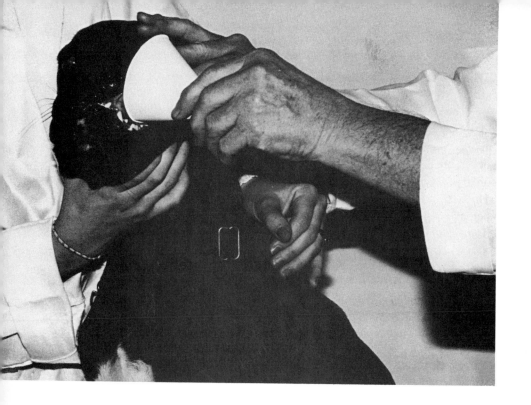

Gently flush it with a solution of one tablespoon of salt to one quart of water (to combat bacterial growth). Next cover the burn with a soft, wet cloth.

Animal bites. Too often bites don't look as bad as they really are. The canine tooth of an animal makes a small hole, but causes a tremendous amount of internal damage and always deposits hair and dirt in the wound.

What you have to do is clip the hair around the bite and use a cotton-tipped swab dipped in petroleum jelly to remove as much foreign matter from the wound as possible. Then apply a first aid cream.

It is extremely important *to keep the wound open*. If you don't, you'll have a large abscess complicating matters. Daily gentle probing with a petrolatum coated swab will keep a wound open, but if there's any sign—any sign at all—of infection after a day or so, see your veterinarian.

Important: If your dog has been bitten by a cat, immediate medical attention is required. With apologies to cat owners who may be reading this, there is no bite more likely to become infected than a cat's bite.

Gunshot wounds. Most of these are caused by birdshot from the gun of an overanxious hunter. Unless a vital organ or bone is hit, such wounds are not a serious problem—except for the initial discomfort and soreness, of course.

When birdshot penetrates the skin, that shot is as sterile as a surgical scalpel. Things get very hot inside the barrel of a shotgun. (Or the barrel of any firearm for that matter.) Many a dog, X-rayed for an unrelated problem, is discovered to have a shot pellet or a small-caliber bullet imbedded in him—history thereof unknown. Sometime, somehow, that animal had been shot. But the thing that caused the wound also sterilized it, and it healed spontaneously.

However, if you are aware of the shooting wound, treat it as you would a superficial or puncture wound. Clip it, clean it, keep it open so it can drain, and *do not* probe for the pellet or bullet. The injury will heal.

The exception here, as might be expected, is a wound caused by a large-caliber rifle. This usually produces sufficient damage to make the need for immediate veterinary care obvious. The only first aid you can give is to apply direct pressure in an effort to control bleeding.

B-B shot. Air guns generate no heat. Therefore, an airgun projectile can cause infection and abscess, whether deeply imbedded or lodged just under the skin. Worse, such pellets are almost impossible to find even with an X-ray. Or two X-rays. Or even three. Those that can't be found will—eventually—come out on their own or, remain where they are, encapsulated in scar tissue.

If you can find the area that was struck, however, treat it as you would a minor scrape, and take your dog to your veterinarian.

Other puncture wounds. Such wounds usually happen as a result of your dog running into or stepping on something. If the injury is minor—a bit of glass or a carpet tack in a paw, for instance—simply remove the tack or glass, let the cut bleed a bit, clean it, and apply a first aid cream.

If the injury is serious, it cannot readily be treated on a first aid basis, and some terrible messes have resulted from attempts to do so. Whatever that foreign object is, leave it where it is, protect yourself from being bitten, and get a veterinarian's help as soon as possible.

Skin allergies. Dogs are subject to hives. They'll get welts on their skin, just as people do. Their faces and lips will get all blown up, just as people's will.

The cause could be an insect bite, a bee sting, making a meal of or coming in contact with certain toadstools, or even suddenly becoming allergic to food that, previously, presented no problem. Regardless of the cause, an injection administered by your veterinarian will alleviate the condition in short order.

Meanwhile, there are a few things you can do to make your dog's life a bit more comfortable.

As long as the animal is breathing normally, its lip membranes are pink, and it does not seem to be distressed except for the itching, an over-the-counter antihistamine tablet or two will help relieve the itch and quiet your dog down. You can also ease the itching with a mild solution of baking soda. But use cool water. Warm water will only make things worse.

Ticks. The direct approach to removing a tick is the best approach.

Don't worry about leaving the pest's head or pincers under the skin. There is no record of a tick ever being separated from its head. If the tick has been on the dog any length of time, it will have created a swelling like a mosquito bite. After a couple of days, the tick bite will become rather hard. Treat that area with a little hydrogen peroxide and a dab of first aid cream.

By the way, a female tick will gorge herself with blood. A male tick won't. This has nothing to do with how you remove or treat either kind. We just thought you'd be interested in knowing how to tell the difference.

Tick removal. Because ticks can carry Rocky Mountain spotted fever and other diseases of serious consequence to humans, we strongly recommend using a pair of tweezers. Grasp the pest by its body and peel it off the surface toward its head. Here again, we've used a human model to demonstrate the technique. (It's a real tick, though.)

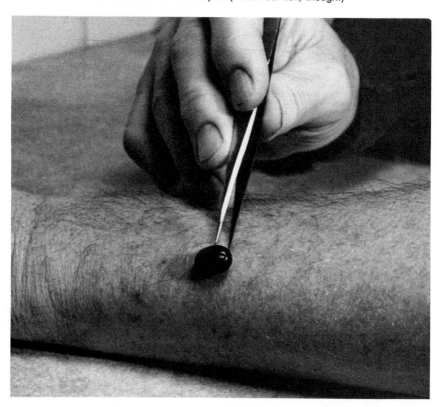

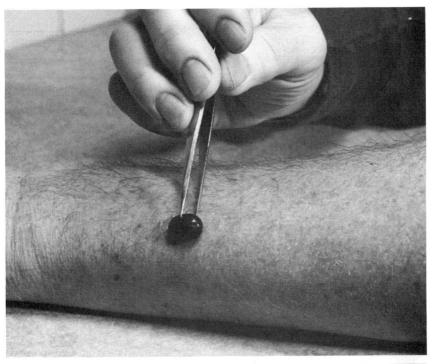

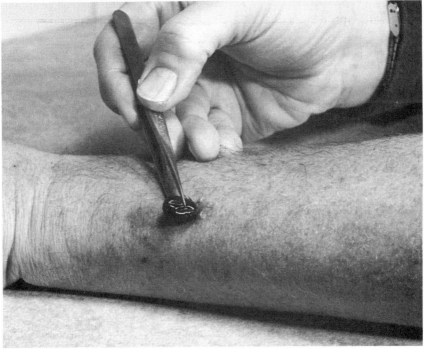

2 THE EYES, THE EARS, THE NOSE, THE MOUTH

Being naturally curious, dogs lead with their noses and are forever getting into trouble because of it. Most emergency problems caused by this tendency, however, could have been prevented by the dog's owner.

How many times have you been driving somehwere and seen a dog—eyes open, tongue out, ears flapping—with its head sticking out the window of another car? The animal looks like it's having the time of its life, but the wind can irritate its eyes, and there are all sorts of foreign bodies floating or flying around out there that can cause even more serious problems.

There are also precautions you should take in and around the house. If you have a fenced-in yard for the dog to run loose in, make certain the fence has no sharp or jagged edges. They can easily tear an ear or puncture an eye.

If you wouldn't leave something lying around that you wouldn't want your child to get into, don't leave it lying around for your dog to get into. An old paintbrush soaking in a can of thinner or cleaner, if knocked over, could cause serious eye burns. The same is true for open containers of insecticides, masonry cleaners, and just about anything else that could cause injury or irritation to a human being.

Controlling your dog's environment is good preventive medicine, and can do a great deal to protect the animal from injuring itself as a result of its natural nosiness.

MAINTAINING GENERAL HEALTH

People should have annual checkups; so should dogs.

One of the biggest problems seen in dogs that aren't examined regularly is periodontal disease. It can raise just as much havoc, or more, with a dog as it can with a human. The disease starts at the gum line, with tartar build-up, then attacks the jawbone, eventually loosening the teeth. Good dental hygiene can prevent it.

Yes, you should brush your dog's teeth. Use a "dog toothpaste" if you

Brushing teeth. Your dentist advises you to brush your gums as well as your teeth. You're advised here to do the same for your dog. Get those lips out of the way, work from front to back or back to front and don't use an angled toothbrush. A flat, wide, straight one will help assure a better cleaning.

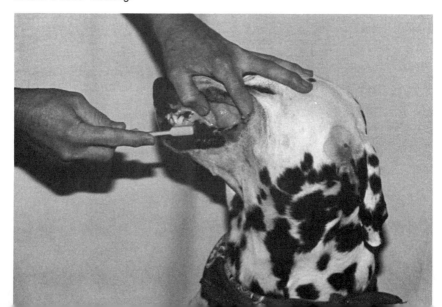

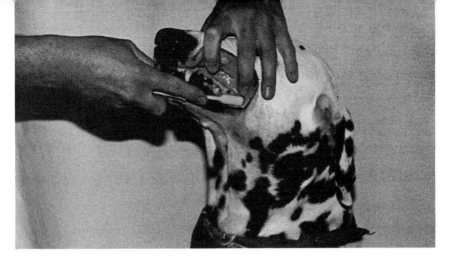

want to. They're available. The act of brushing with plain water, perhaps with a little salt or baking soda added, is sufficient to clean them, however.

No, dog biscuits won't clean your dog's gums. Dogs don't chew with their gums, and dog biscuits won't keep tartar from building up there. Biscuits might serve to break some buildup of tartar on the teeth, but that's about all.

Some breeds are more prone to eye problems than others: the peke, pug,

boxer, or any other dog with prominent eyes; the poodle, or any other dog with a lot of hair around the eyes. Daily care in keeping the area around the eyes clean and the corners wiped out with warm water can prevent many eye problems from ever arising with such animals.

If your dog has prominent eyes, be it a purebred or otherwise, go easy on the roughhousing. And tell any children who come in contact with the animal to do the same. Merely pulling too hard on a choke collar can literally pop the eyes of a prominently eyed dog right out of their sockets.

Floppy-eared dogs and dogs with a lot of hair inside their ears should have them checked and cleaned daily. Yes, daily. You wash and dry them as you would your own ears. Using a mild dishwashing detergent—any brand that's kind to your hands—rather than cake soap helps to reduce wax buildup. Don't worry about getting a little water in your dog's ear during the cleaning process. Its ability to rid itself of such trapped moisture by shaking its head is far greater than yours.

SPECIFIC INJURIES

The Eye

Eye irritants. The dog riding with its head out the car window can have its eyeballs dried out by the wind. Soap, aerosols of any kind—including your spray-on deodorant—can inflame and irritate the eye.

If you're on the scene, immediately flush the eye with contact lens solution, artifical tears, or even plain water.

Once flushed—and sometimes that's all that's necessary—use a commercial eye wash or light mineral oil to soothe and protect the eye(s).

You must keep the animal from pawing at its irritated eye(s). Cuddle, hold, and stroke your dog. If that doesn't work, wrap a large towel around its neck. With mild irritations, the crisis is usually over in about fifteen minutes.

Eye washing. Whether you use a special eye wash or plain water, saturate a clean cloth with it. Gently holding your dog's head, hold the cloth over the eye and squeeze the liquid directly on the affected area. Repeat until the irritant has been thoroughly flushed out.

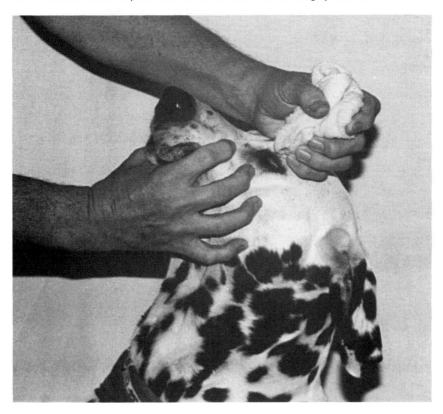

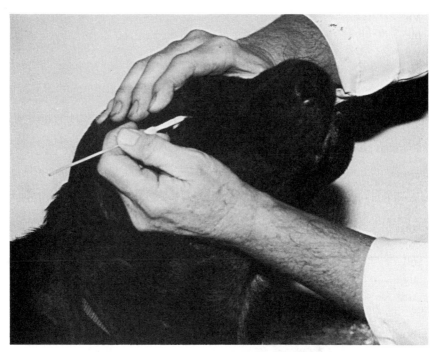

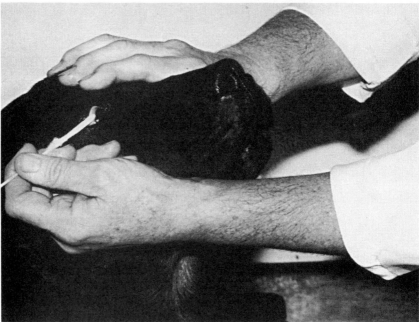

Removing foreign body from eye. A wet napkin or tissue can be used. However, a wet, cotton swab is better. Secure the animal's head. Force the upper lid up and gently wipe the foreign body off the surface of the eyeball.

Visible foreign body. If you can actually see that grain of sand, bit of dirt, or piece of grass on the surface of the eyeball, you can remove it yourself. But if you're going to do it—do it! In seconds. Even though most dogs are more cooperative under such circumstances than a five-year-old child, don't dawdle. If you give the dog a chance to realize what you're up to, it's going to make a simple task a whole lot tougher.

Unseen foreign body. If you can't see it, there's nothing you can do about it from a first aid standpoint. Your next step should be a visit to your veterinarian.

There is something you should know about such an eye injury, however: the third eyelid. (Official name: Nictitan's membrane). It's located in the nose corner of the eye. Irritation from a foreign body causes the membrane to come up and cover the eye, making it appear as though your dog's eye had rolled back in its socket. When and if the membrane appears, it serves to suggest there's something in your dog's eye that requires medical attention. And the sooner it receives it, the better.

Skunks and other severe irritants. Close encounters with odorous black-and-white bushy-tailed mammals, gasoline, kerosene, and mace all burn the cornea.

The eye, or eyes, must be immediately flushed with mineral oil—not water—while the dog is restrained. In every case, these severe eye irritations will cause secondary problems that can only be treated by a veterinarian.

Wounds. A scratch on the eyeball itself, regardless of the cause, must have a veterinarian's care. The only first aid for such injuries is to apply a commercial eye wash or mineral oil to the eye to soothe it. *Do not* touch the eye. *Do not* wash it out with water.

Punctures or ruptures. These are indicated by fluid actually oozing out of the eyeball itself. Far more serious than a scratch, these injuries require *immediate* medical attention.

Your dog will be very disturbed and will insist on pawing at its eye, which will only damage it further. You *must* keep it from doing so, even if it means taping or tieing the animal's legs together.

If the eye has been punctured, leave whatever punctured it alone—expecially if the object is a fish hook.

If the eye is ruptured, don't touch it.

Apply a commercial eyewash or light mineral oil to soothe the injury, and transport your dog to the veterinarian.

Hemorrhages. Although it looks very dramatic and is upsetting to both you and your dog, keep calm. The bleeding usually isn't coming from the eye itself, but from the tissues around the eye.

Apply cold compress to control the bleeding. You dog may end up with the equivalent of a shiner, but the eye hasn't been damaged.

Popped out of socket. As we said earlier, this is most likely to occur to dogs with prominent eyes. It is *not* the end of the world.

Unless great ripping and tearing of muscles accompanies the injury, the eye can be replaced and can function.

Protect the eye by gently smearing it with plain petroleum jelly or a soluble lubricating jelly, such as K-Y jelly, and cover it with a cool, wet, nonlinty cloth.

In most cases, you will not have to restrain your dog since it will be rather tranquil due to mild shock. If the eye is to be saved, however, getting the animal to a veterinarian right after first aid is given is a matter of urgency.

Allergic reactions. If one of your dog's eyes is swollen shut, it might be an allergic reaction. (It might also be due to a foreign body or scratch that escaped earlier detection). If both eyes are swollen shut, it's more than likely an allergic reaction. In which case, the problem isn't in the eye but in the tissues around it.

In any case, apply cold compresses, over-the-counter ointments containing antihistamine and cortisone, and call your veterinarian.

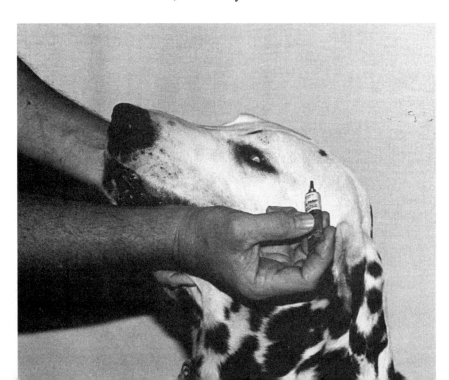

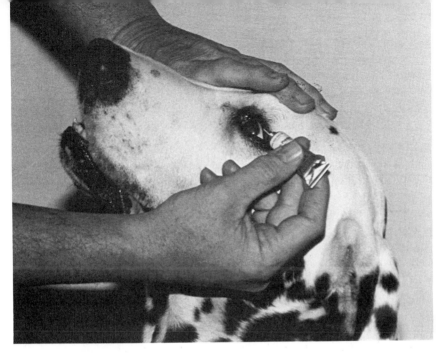

Applying eye medication. Hold your dog's jaws closed and its head still. Apply the ointment, cream, or drops inside the outer edge of the eye. Then, gently massage the upper lid over the eyeball. Doing so will cause the medication to be distributed over the eyeball where it will do the most good.

The Ear

Acute inflammation. One day your dog is fine. The next it's shaking it head frequently and/or rubbing its ear on the ground. There's possibly a foreign body in there.

Gently sponge water into the ear, wipe it out, then do it again until you can see what's causing the problem.

Once you have it spotted, use a pair of tweezers to get it out. If it's a tick, remove it as shown in Chapter 1, pages 14–15.

Infections. Your dog didn't get an ear infection this morning. They take time to develop.

Once one has set in, it's painful. There is a very unpleasant odor, and your dog is obviously unhappy.

Flush the ear out with warm water and mild soap, dry it as thoroughly as you can, then apply ointment containing cortisone or antihistamine. If the condition doesn't soon improve, call your veterinarian.

A Reminder: When you wash your dog, don't ever leave soap in its ears. The residue can easily lead to the type of infection just described.

Wounds. Because of the tremendous blood supply in the ear, even a minor wound will bleed profusely. You dog will greatly aid and abet the bleeding by constantly shaking its head in annoyance. Nine out of ten times, ear wounds are going to need stitching, but first aid first.

Apply direct pressure to the wound to arrest bleeding. (Using a styptic pencil often helps.) Clean the area with hydrogen peroxide, then hold a dry cotton ball on the wound until it sticks there. Next, you have to secure your dog's ears so they can't be shaken and undo what you have just done.

Securing the ears. Fold a T-shirt or clean dish towel into a strip long enough to go around your dog's head. Wrap the cloth around the head, enclosing the ears, and secure it in place with adhesive or masking tape.

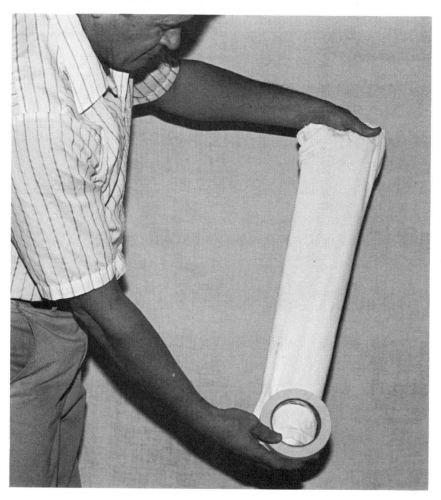

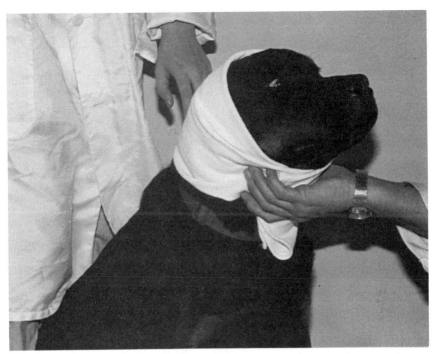

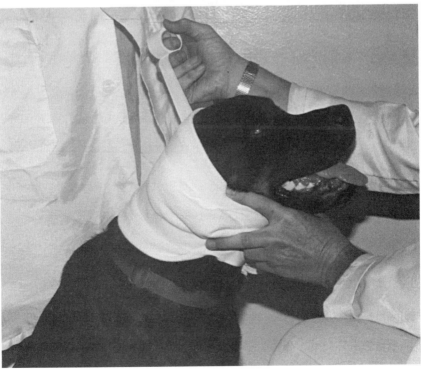

Mites. Mites are little insects that cause mange. Mites in the ear cause mange of the ear.

The itching is intense, and your dog will naturally scratch at it constantly.

You can give the animal temporary relief by flushing out its ears with tepid water and applying a cortisone ointment, but the only cure is with your veterinarian.

The Nose

There isn't much first aid you can apply to a dog's nose. But there's some.

Discharges of mucus from both nostrils. This may be temporarily relieved by giving the animal cold medicine as prescribed in Chapter 12.

Discharges from one nostril. This might indicate there's a foreign object present—which you should leave to your veterinarian to remove.

Cut nose. These will bleed heavily. Cold compresses and direct pressure can stop the bleeding, but any size cut on the nose will probably require stitches.

Sudden nose bleed. If the animal begins to bleed from the nose for no apparent reason—most common with older dogs—this is a sign of bad teeth. Again, cold compresses and direct pressure can be applied, but a veterinarian's attention is usually required.

The Mouth

Foreign body. The signs are drooling, pawing at the mouth, and rubbing the face. Most frequently, the foreign body will be a stick or bone.

Pull it out by all means, but you can't be sure you've gotten it all out.

Even if the main object dislodges itself, there may be slivers or splinters of it left behind, which will result in abscess if not removed. Have your veterinarian take a closer look.

Fish hooks. There's absolutely no safe way you, personally, can remove a fish hook. Don't even try. And don't let anyone else try.

If it's attached to a line, cut the line off six inches or so from the eye of the hook and be on your way to a veterinarian.

Bones. Dogs should not be given bones they can chew up or get entirely into their mouth. Bones, all bones, are indigestible.

Ring bones, as in ham, can get hooked over a dog's lower jaw, and they won't come off until they're cut off.

Rib bones can get gnawed down to a size that allows them to become wedged across the roof of a dog's mouth. If you don't spot them, you'll soon begin to smell them.

If your dog *must* be given something to chew on besides its food, dog biscuits, rawhide "toys," or even an old bedroom slipper are far better for it—and a lot less risky—than bones.

String. If your dog tries to make a meal of it, and part of that meal is dangling from its mouth, *do not* follow your natural urge and yank it away. Instead pull on it gently.

If there's any resistance, stop at once. It's too late for you to get it out from inside your dog, and the task must be left up to a veterinarian.

Oral bleeding. The most common cause is bad teeth, but dogs bleed from the mouth for other and sometimes unexplainable reasons.

Try to flush the mouth with cool water, but if the bleeding's caused by a tooth, the tooth will have to come out.

If the hemorrhage is caused by a laceration outside the mouth, it will eventually stop as a result of your applying pressure to the affected area.

Daubing on a bit of first aid cream or plain petroleum jelly will soothe things somewhat, but keep your eyes peeled for signs of infection.

Porcupines. The quill of the porcupine is nature's first fish hook. If there are any quills present—and you can restrain your dog while resigning yourself to the fact that you're going to hurt it—quick yanks with a pair of long-nose pliers will remove them.

But not necessarily their barbs. Eventually, nature will take care of those. There are many, many dogs happily running around to prove it.

If the number of quills is large, though, and you can't get to a veterinarian, only attempt to remove those close to the eyes, nose, and inside the mouth.

The remaining quills *will* fall out after a time. Waiting for them to do so won't be very comfortable for your dog or very easy on you, but fall out they will.

3 THE HEART, THE LUNGS, AND CPR

The cause of congestive heart failure in dogs is the same as it is in humans. When, for any reason, the heart is unable to pump strongly enough to supply blood to the lungs, fluid collects in the lungs. The fluid reduces the lung's ability to deliver oxygen to the bloodstream. One problem compounds the other. The heart weakens further. The lungs deliver less oxygen. The heart stops.

Heart failure, human and canine, happens most often among the older of both species, but it can be prevented—or at least postponed—by early detection and treatment. Older people are encouraged to get annual checkups. Owners of older dogs are here encouraged to see that their pets get the same. There are special diets and cardiopulmonary exercise programs for senior citizens. There are special diets and similar programs for senior canines as well.

EARLY WARNING SIGNALS

Your dog will cough frequently, particularly after a period of excitement or exercise. The animal will tend toward less and less activity, tire easily, and pant more than usual under any kind of stress. Eventually, the fluid accumulating in its lungs will do likewise in the abdominal cavity and obviously distend the stomach.

If you fail to notice these signs and don't seek veterinary care, be prepared for what is to come by reading, and rereading, what follows.

SPECIFIC PROBLEMS/INJURIES

Congestive heart failure. The animal is in a sitting position. Its head is elevated. It is gasping for breath. Its inner lip membranes are blue.

Your dog's condition is critical. Any chance of survival depends on your moving it, gently and very quickly, to your veterinarian. During transport, maintain the animal in a sitting position, keep it relatively cool, and give it no medication, no water, no ice cubes or stimulants of any kind.

Lungs, punctured: open wound. Such injuries are called "sucking wounds," since you can hear the air rushing into and out of the chest cavity. Cover the opening with a wet cloth, bandage to secure the cloth in place, lay the animal on its injured side, and transport it to your veterinarian.

Lungs, functured: foreign body. No matter what it is, don't try to pull it out! Seal off the area immediately *around* the object as best you can with a wet cloth, then bandage the area *around* the object to secure the cloth. Take extreme care not to force the foreign body in deeper during the trip to the veterinarian.

Lungs: electric shock. Besides treating the burns resulting from an electric shock as discussed in Chapter 2, be alert for deeper damage. In this case, damage to the lungs and a buildup of fluid in the lung tissue itself. The medical term for this is pulmonary edema. What it does is cause drowning on dry land.

If the dog is conscious, keep it calm and in a sitting position with its head extended while you take it to a veterinarian without delay.

If the dog is unconscious, keep its head extended and maintain an open airway by holding its mouth open and pulling its tongue to one side. *Administer artificial respiration as shown opposite.* Once the animal has regained consciousness, get medical help immediately.

Heat stroke. The animal has collapsed and is hyperventilating. Cool it down. Fast. Sitting your dog in a tub of ice water is the fastest, but spraying it with a cold hose will do. If the animal is conscious and able to swallow, let it lick ice cubes on the way to the veterinarian.

Note: Of all crises involving a dog's cardiopulmonary system, this one can, should, and ought to be avoided.

Never leave your dog in a closed car on a hot day.

Never choose a hot day to run your dog ragged chasing a Frisbee or ball or indulging in some other form of excessive exercise.

Never tie your dog outdoors on a hot day unless a shady area is close enough to shelter the animal from the heat. No, a dog house doesn't count as a shady area unless it's *in* the shade. If it's not, it's hotter in there than it is in the sun.

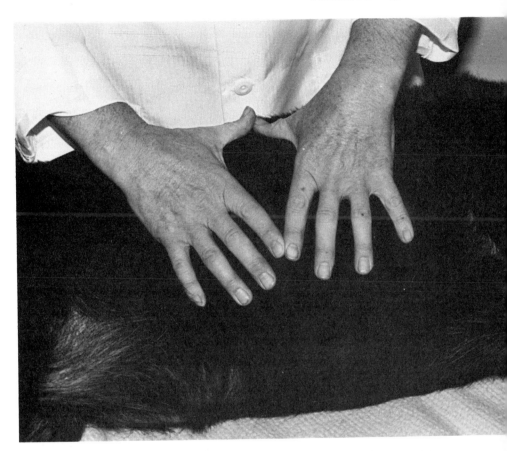

CPR. Place both hands on the dog's rib cage with fingers spread as shown. Now press down and release, press down and release. Keep a steady rhythm. When you release, release quickly and completely. What you're trying to do is pump air into and out of your dog's lungs and, at the same time, stimulate heart action.

4

CHICKEN SOUP
AND THE
DIGESTIVE SYSTEM

Some dogs will eat almost anything, creating problems for themselves and their owners. Once the animal has swallowed whatever-it-is, first aid is quite limited.

Preventive measures, however, are not. Most obvious among them is a balanced diet.

In Chapter 1, we talked about commercial dog foods versus home cooking. What was said then bears repeating. You can't prepare food for your dog as well as dog food companies so. They know dogs can't handle spices or high fat foods and can't even digest bones. They do a tremendous amount of research into canine nutrition and include what they discover in their products. With the one or two exceptions covered later on in this chapter, there's nothing you can whip up in your kitchen that's going to provide your dog with a better balanced diet than the food you buy in any supermarket.

The only person who knows more than a commercial dog food manufacturer about your dog's *individual* dietary needs is your veterinarian.

Another preventive measure, seemingly obvious, is to keep your dog away from garbage—yours and your neighbor's. The remains of people food may be tempting to your dog's nose, but it creates problems once it reaches the stomach.

SPECIFIC PROBLEMS—FOREIGN BODIES

Upper throat. The most common problem—as with the mouth—is with sticks, bits of bone, and string becoming lodged in the throat. If the object is visible, just aft of the tongue, you may be able to reach back in there and dislodge it. You'll have to put a gag in your dog's mouth first, though—demonstrated on page 36.

One caution and two definite "dont's," mentioned earlier, bear repeating. If the object is a string, and it comes out after a *gentle* pull, fine. But *don't* get into a tug-of-war with it. If the object is a fish hook or barbed in any way, *don't* touch it. Stubborn pieces of string and barbed foreign bodies are objects for a veterinarian to remove.

Gag. Use a roll of tape, a roll of gauze, or a rubber ball to prop open your dog's jaws. With the gag in place—we've removed it here to better illustrate the next step—reach in with two fingers, grasp the object between them and remove it. *Remember*, if it's a piece of string and doesn't come out easily, give up trying. If it's hooked or barbed in any way, *don't touch it!*

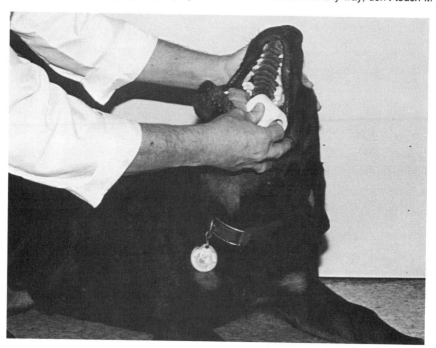

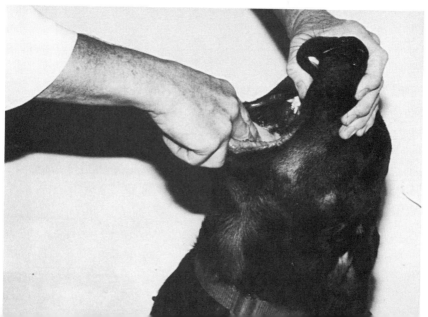

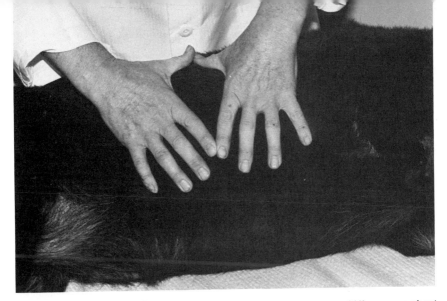

Heimlich maneuver. Place your hands on the dog's rib cage as you would if you were about to administer CPR. Push down *sharply*, very *quickly* and *firmly, then release just as quickly.* Keep it up. Think of your dog's lungs as a bellows you're using to try to force out the object stuck in its throat.

Down the throat. If there's something stuck in the animal's throat, your dog will gag, drool, and paw at its muzzle. If the object is down there far enough, there may be some interference with the dog's breathing, and its inner lip membranes will acquire a distinct bluish color due to lack of oxygen in the bloodstream. You can't reach in after the object, but you can perform a canine version of the Heimlich maneuver in an effort to dislodge it.

Esophagus. When what has been swallowed gets this far down, your dog will drool consistently. There will be frequent gagging and some abortive vomiting. If the object has become lodged near the heart, breathing will be difficult, and bluish inner lip membranes will be evident. You can try to dislodge the object with the Heimlich maneuver shown above. If that is unsuccessful, as it most often is in this case, your dog is going to need a veterinarian.

Stomach. If you see your dog swallow something, and it's not sharp, try to make the animal throw up. There are three ways to do so that work and work quickly.

1. Force the dog to swallow hydrogen peroxide, three to four teaspoons. 2. Force it to swallow a strong salt-water solution. 3. Stick your finger down its throat.

If your dog swallows something and the something has sharp edges or points, *don't* attempt to make the animal throw up. There might be internal

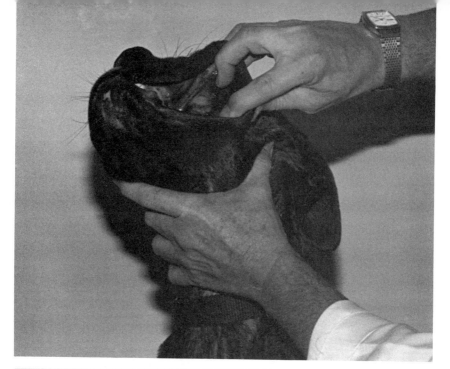

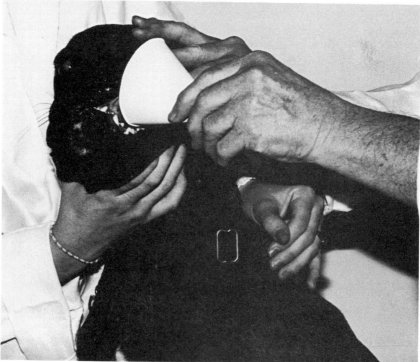

Forced swallowing to induce vomiting. Hold open the pocket between your dog's teeth and lips at the rear of its jaw. Hold its mouth closed while you pour in the hydrogen peroxide or salt water solution.

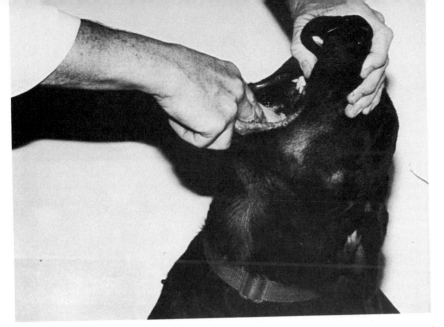

Inducing vomiting with fingers. Hold your dog's upper jaw in one hand. Use two fingers of the other hand to open its mouth, then slide them back over the tongue far enough to induce gagging. Be careful not to pinch the animal's lips against its teeth. The dog's natural reaction to your doing so could result in your fingers needing immediate medical attention.

lacerations in the chest area which can only be made worse by muscle spasms of vomiting.

Usually, however, you don't see the foreign body get swallowed. What then?

After its next meal, or even a day or two later, your dog will throw up all by itself and completely lose interest in food. You can give it any over-the-counter stomach coating emulsion—the same you'd take if you'd overdosed on pepperoni pizza—and withhold food and water for a day. If the throwing up persists, see your veterinarian.

Small intestine. There will be persistent vomiting after eating—if your dog is still eating. The constant throwing up will cause dehydration. You can make things a little easier for the animal by giving it a stomach soothing emulsion. If the object is sharp, however, the vomiting will be accompanied by severe adbominal pain, and the dog requires immediate veterinary attention.

Large intestine. Usually, once a foreign body has reached the colon, the dog will pass it. A long object—a piece of string, for example—may not pass all at once. If you notice it protruding from the animal's anus, cut off the part you can see, but do not attempt to remove it. You don't know where the other end is. If the object hasn't passed completely in twenty-four to forty-eight hours, see your veterinarian.

DIGESTIVE PROBLEMS

Vomiting and diarrhea: acute onset. One day your dog is fine, the next it's obviously sick—probably because it's eaten something it shouldn't have.

First, you have to stop the vomiting. Withhold all food and water, and give your dog a stomach-coating agent. If the coating agent gets thrown up, administer another dose. keep doing the same until you have the vomiting under control. Once it is, you can attend to the diarrhea.

Now you can cook for your dog.

Chicken soup, with the fat skimmed off, will do more to cure your dog's diarrhea than it is purported to do for all human ills.

You can also prepare more solid foods. A mixture of boiled rice and nongreasy hamburger, perhaps. Or boiled rice and chicken with the skin removed.

None of the above is to be accompanied by the traditional bowl of water. Replace it with two or three ice cubes, held in your hand, that your dog can lick on.

Vomiting and diarrhea: prolonged. If the treatment described above fails to clear up the problem, traces of blood will eventually show themselves. As long as they remain traces, they're not necessarily alarming, but if they are excessive, calling your veterinarian is definitely in order.

Colic. It happens with babies, it happens with dogs. Particularly with puppies who have been overfed or fed the wrong thing—too much whole milk, for instance.

These severe stomach cramps may be accompanied by mild stomach distension. Don't give the animal any food or water. Do give it one or two spoonfuls of your favorite stomach-coating agent. If the crisis passes, ease the dog back to its regular diet by feeding and watering it as described in acute onset, (above). Should the dog be a puppy, you can substitute strained baby food for the rice, hamburger, and chicken.

If the colic continues for any length of time, see your veterinarian. You may be dealing with something far more serious than stomach cramps.

Bloat. Of all digestive problems, this is the most serious. With larger dogs, it is serious enough to cause death.

The cause of bloat is still under dispute, so we won't speculate here. Its symptoms are obvious. There is severe distress and obvious distension of the abdomen. There is drooling and abortive vomiting, and the animal will pace constantly in search of relief.

Withhold all food and water. Give the dog one or two drugstore variety antiacid/antigas tablets. If relief is not immediate, consult your veterinarian posthaste.

Note: To help avoid bloat in large dogs, feed them smaller amounts more often rather than one big meal, and avoid a lot of activity right after eating.

Constipation. You have a choice of things to do, but whichever you decide on, you can only do it once. If it doesn't work and your dog is still having trouble, see you veterinarian.

Give the dog mineral oil: one teaspoon for a small dog, one or two tablespoons for a large dog. Lacking mineral oil, administer milk of magnesia mixed with whole milk. See Chapter 12 for dosage.

Feed it liver, even if it means opening a can of liver-based cat food.

Insert a suppository if it's a small dog—in which case you may need help.

Give it an enema if it's a large dog—in which case you will definitely need help.

Anal glands (sacs). These are located at four and eight o'clock in the anal tissue and have no known useful function in the modern dog. At times, they become blocked up and infected. When they do, your dog will make you aware of the fact by dragging its backside along the rug or floor.

If you somehow overlook or miss your dog's signs of distress, the sacs may abscess, rupture, and start to bleed.

Soothe the area with a wet, warm compress, apply a commercial hemorrhoid medication, and gently squeeze the glands in an attempt to clean them out.

Wash the area, apply hydrogen peroxide, dry the area, and apply first aid cream.

After administering first aid, take your dog to your veterinarian.

5 THE URINARY TRACT

Very few emergency-type problems arise from your dog's ability—or inability—to urinate, but we'll discuss a few considerations.

Once a day is not enough. In order to maintain normal function, you must provide regular exercise periods during the course of a day. Notice, "periods." A morning walk or jog, followed by nothing until the next morning walk or job, doesn't offer your dog sufficient opportunity to relieve itself. The older the dog happens to be, the more frequent will be the need for relief.

Access to fresh water. It's a must—at all times. If you forget to provide water, your dog's need will drive it into the bathroom and the toilet bowl. Even if you use no chemicals in the bowl, your dog should not drink from it. Dogs are subject to the same bacterial infections as people.

Be aware of your dog's drinking habits. Watch for sudden changes in intake, either up or down. If they persist for two or three days, it may be a warning signal of diabetes, kidney problems, or infection. All of which are treatable by your veterinarian.

SPECIFIC PROBLEMS

Difficulty in urinating. This is usually common in the male dog. The animal strains to relieve itself but can't. The most frequent cause is a blockage due to bladder stones and/or urethral stones.

Determine whether this is an emergency by gently pushing from side to side with your fingers just in front of the dog's hindquarters. If you feel something like an orange or grapefruit in there, and the dog resents your attentions, the emergency exists and requires immediate veterinarian care.

If you don't feel anything and the dog doesn't resent your action, an early blockage is present, and you have a little time before going to your veterinarian. In which case, give the animal aspirin or buffered aspirin to reduce its discomfort.

Small, frequent amounts. This is not necessarily a blockage. However, when frequent urination is accompanied by a strong odor, it could indicate a bladder infection. Give aspirin or buffered aspirin, encourage the dog to drink more water, and when you take it to your veterinarian, take a urine sample with you.

Blood in urine. This occurs most often in males and indicates an inflammation of the prostate gland—usually because there is a female in heat somewhere in the neighborhood. However, the condition is also present in elderly dogs.

The problem can clear up as quickly as it showed up. Meanwhile, aspirin, buffered or not, and free access to water can relieve discomfort.

It it continues, it may indicate a bladder infection, ongoing prostatitis, the formation of stones, or a tumor. Plan to see your veterinarian in the very near future.

The Monday-morning bladder. This only happens to dogs who have been well housebroken and whose owners have gone away for the weekend, leaving it abundant food and water. Because the animal knows going in the house is a no-no, it doesn't. The distended bladder becomes inflamed, and when relief finally comes, there may be blood in the urine.

You can give the animal aspirin or buffered aspirin to reduce the inflammation. Next time you go away, hire a dog sitter or put the animal in a kennel, and thus totally avoid the problem.

The foul-weather bladder. The cause is a combination of well-housebroken dog, cold, rain, or snow, and a strong desire on the part of both owner and dog not to go ourside.

The result is a bladder inflammation. This is treatable with aspirin or buffered aspirin, but it is best by far to prevent it ever happening in the first place: *No matter how lousy it is out there, take the dog out.*

6

SEIZURES
AND FAINTING

There are almost as many kinds of seizures as there are causes for seizures. All are related to brain malfuction. This can result from a bump on the head, lack of oxygen, low blood sugar, low blood calcium, poisons, and tumors of the brain. In young puppies, viral attacks on brain cells can cause seizures—unless the attacks are prevented by distemper shots.

SEIZURES

The mild seizure. This is so unobtrusive that you might not even notice it's happening. Your dog will be almost catatonic, as though in a hypnotic trance. The animal will stare into space and be more or less "out of it."

There's little to do but wait for the spell to pass—which it usually does in a short period of time.

The petit mal. All of the above will occur, plus drooling, panting, and slight muscle tremors.

As with a mild seizure, the animal should recover spontaneously within a few minutes.

The grand mal. The dog is down, drooling, panting, stiffened, making running motions, and thrashing, and it has lost control of its bladder and bowels. *The grand mal is the only form of seizure you can approach from a first aid standpoint.*

1. If the seizure is taking place close to a fireplace, stove, or other object that could cause further injury, gently grasp the dog by the scruff of the neck and drag it away to a safe spot.

2. Don't try to yell or slap the dog out of it. Doing so could intensify the attack.

3. Give no fluids. Administer no medication. Trying to get anything down

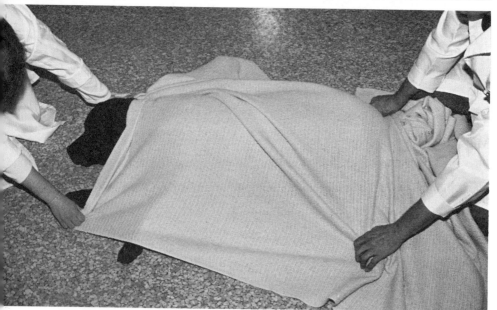

Blanket restraint for seizures. As a result of its seizure, the animal is already down. Immobilize it as best you can by placing a blanket over it and holding the blanket against the floor as close to the dog's body as possible.

the throat of a dog experiencing a grand mal can easily cost your a finger.

4. Restrain the animal by putting a blanket over it and holding the blanket down, not the dog.

Most grand mals don't last more than a few moments, but are exhausting for both dog and owner. Coming out of it, your dog will be confused, bewildered, and disoriented. Give it time to recover. When the animal is obviously more aware of its surroundings—of you and of itself—let it have an ice cube to lick. Quite often, one seizure is the end of it, and there's no need at the moment to see a veterinarian.

However, if the dog goes into another seizure immediately, or if the one it's just been through lasted five minutes or more, the need for veterinary care is urgent.

FAINTING

The dog has collasped. It is not convulsing and cannot be wakened. Its eyes will be open. Sleeping dogs close their eyes, unconscious dogs don't.

The deeper the unconscious state, the more serious the problem.

Near-conscious. Shine a light in the animal's eyes. Do the pupils react to it?

Gently touch the eyeball. Does the eyelid blink?

Pinch a paw. Is it pulled away?

Raise the lips and look at the gums. Are they pink? Is respiration obvious?

The more of these signs you observe, the less unconscious your dog. Leave it alone. It should come out of it on its own.

Mid-conscious. You receive no reaction to the above tests, the lip membranes aren't a healthy pink, but breathing is obvious.

Check for a heartbeat by placing your fingers on the dog's chest behind its foreleg, give the animal CPR (shown on page 33), and see your veterinarian.

Critically unconscious. You receive no reaction to the tests, lip membranes are blue, eyes are glazed, there is no visible respiration, and you cannot detect a heartbeat. In all probability, bladder and bowel control will have been lost. *You only have minutes to get your dog to a veterinarian, and you must administer CPR constantly during transit.*

The chances for survival are very, very slim.

7 PARASITES

Parasites are not an emergency problem, but they can and do create emergencies. The more you know about these pests, the better you'll be able to avoid an emergency ever happening, so consider what follows preventive medicine and practice it.

INTERNAL PARASITES

Roundworm. Most common in young puppies, roundworms can enter the body before birth. The mother harbors the larvae in her system. If not detected by veterinary care, the larvae migrate through the young animal's system, enter the lungs, penetrate, and travel up the windpipe. As a result, the larvae get swallowed and mature in the stomach, reaching the size of a pencil.

A typical sign of roundworm is a pot-bellied, undernourished puppy, who should be taken to a veterinarian where the cause of its condition can be cured.

Hookworm. Almost microscopic, hookworms are more serious in puppies than in adult dogs.

These pests actually attach themselves to the intestinal wall and draw blood, causing anemia and diarrhea. With a healthy adult animal, there's a certain amount of resistance, even immunity. The dog's system can actually encapsulate the larvae so they don't mature.

Hookworms are most commonly passed from dog to dog via feces. The eggs are in the feces and produce larvae. A dog coming in contact with the feces or contaminated soil may ingest the eggs or larvae. The larvae have the ability to enter by puncturing the skin. The majority of commercial, granular insecticides will kill hookworm larvae on your lawn, and you should make a habit of keeping the area your dog runs around in policed up.

Whipworm. More often found in adult dogs, whipworms live in the lower bowel. They cause intermittent diarrhea. One bowel movement will be normal, the next will be watery with mucus. If allowed to continue, the condition will debilitate your dog due to dehydration.

Whipworm, like hookworm, is passed from dog to dog. The larvae are encapsulated in a tough shell and can survive for years in the soil. Again, good sanitation of your dog's "turf" is required to help prevent infection.

Heartworm. About the size and shape of spaghetti, heartworms, as their name indicates, live in the heart.

Obviously, a bunch of spaghetti in the heart is going to interfere with its function, eventually causing pulmonary congestion, habitual coughing, and fluid buildup in the lungs.

If your dog doesn't have the stamina it used to have and is experiencing difficulty breathing, it may have heartworms and will need medical help.

These parasites are not transmitted dog to dog. Not directly. Their microscopic larvae enter the bloodstream of an infected dog. If that dog is bitten by a mosquito, the insect sucks up the larvae during its gorging and carries them to the next dog it bites.

Fortunately, heartworm is easily prevented with medication available from your veterinarian. Annual blood tests and examinations are recommended.

Tapeworm. If you want your dog to be free of tapeworm, keep it free of fleas.

What the mosquito is to heartworm, the flea is to the tapeworm. A segment of the worm within is easily seen on the outside of an infected animal's stool. These segments, about half an inch long, contain the egg. The egg is eaten by a flea. Flea bites dog. Dog bites flea. Dog swallows flea—and egg—and another tapeworm grows.

Medication will eliminate the worm, but treatment won't be necessary if you eliminate the flea. Regular stool analysis by your veterinarian is also recommended.

EXTERNAL PARASITES

Fleas. Being the host for a tapeworm isn't enough. Not for the flea. It causes bite allergies, rash, and secondary bacterial infections resulting from your dog scratching itself raw in agitation.

A veterinarian can treat the allergies. You can sooth any raw areas with a first aid cream or ointment—but treating a dog for fleas is like melting the tip of the iceberg.

Fleas live anywhere from two weeks to over two years, survive severe climatic changes, cannot be casually drowned—not even in salt water—and spend less than 5 percent of their time actually on your dog. To be rid of them, you have to treat dog, home, and property. What you should safely use to do so is a subject to be discussed with your veterinarian.

Ticks. The removal of a tick was discussed in Chapter 1, pages 14–15, and the technique for doing so shown.

Two of the reasons for removing them have not been mentioned: tick fever and tick paralysis. Both are extremely serious and require immediate veterinary attention.

But plucking off the tick and killing it only reduces the tick population by one. Like fleas, ticks are tough. Or tougher. They are extremely resistant to most insecticides, and many of those they're not resistant to are too dangerous to use on your dog.

Ticks lurk in shrubs and bushes waiting for a meal to pass by. It's there you should attack them—by spraying. But consult your veterinarian before you choose what you spray them with.

Lice. They're whitish blue, they like warm light, and when exposed to it, they can easily be spotted with a hand-held magnifying glass.

Dog lice are purely superficial creatures. They don't burrow, they dislike all other animals, including humans, are found mostly on young puppies, and are the result of less than good sanitation.

If your dog has them, give it a good medicated shampooing as recommended by your veterinarian and get rid of its bedding.

Mange mites. Mites don't jump or fly from dog to dog. There has to be contact.

All mites are microscopic creatures. They bite, cause dandruff, inflammation, and loss of hair. One type lives only in the ears, most commonly the ears of younger dogs.

The conditions caused by mites are treatable by a veterinarian and, in some cases, by yourself.

The Demodex mite is cigar-shaped, has little, nonfunctional legs, and lives in the hair follicle. It produces patchy hair loss with no irritation in the early stages. But if the condition is not an isolated one—which can easily be treated by a veterinarian—treatment may be lifelong, due to a breakdown in the animal's immune system.

The Sarcoptes mite is larger than the ear mite. It's a kind of super crab. It scurries about the surface, the female of the species burrowing to lay eggs, and causes the afflicted dog to scratch heavily. Treatable by a veterinarian, Sarcoptes mites are mildly contageous to people. The good news is they tend not to remain with a human host for long.

The dandruff mite produces an inordinate amount of the dry little flakes of skin it's named for and is gotten rid of with mild medicated shampooing. It is not contagious to humans, whose dandruff problems may be plentiful, but cannot be blamed on mites.

8 TRAVELING WITH YOUR DOG

Taking an automobile trip with a well-trained dog can be better than taking one with people. Your dog won't tell you you're going the wrong way. Your dog won't smoke. Your dog won't constantly want to stop, to shop, or sightsee.

You train a dog to travel when it's a puppy. Start with short trips. Around the block or to the store is far enough to get the animal used to the idea and for you to establish its place inside the car.

Once it gets accustomed to riding—and we'll cover what you can do if it doesn't—you can take your dog on long trips.

1. If those trips happen to call for an overnight stay, make sure that the motel or hotel where you reserve accommodations also has accommodations for, or will welcome, your dog.

2. Never confine your pet to the car while you're elsewhere getting a good night's sleep.

3. Children are encouraged to go to the bathroom immediately prior to setting out on a trip. Encourage your dog to do the same by exercising it just before it gets into the car.

4. Attach a leash to your dog's collar and leave it attached. Think of it as a canine safety belt, which can be grabbed in case of a sudden stop—or to keep the animal from bolting the car during a scheduled stop. *Do not tie the leash to anything inside the car.*

5. Provide good ventilation, but do not let the dog ride with its head out the window. If you want to review why you shouldn't, turn to Chapter 2, pages 17 and 21, and reread about eye injuries.

6. Don't let the dog sleep on the floor. Exhaust fumes collect there.

7. Carry a container of ice cubes aboard. If the dog seems restless, give it one to lick. The cube tends to occupy the fidgety one's mind while eliminating any thirst.

8. For feeding en route, use semimoist, packaged food in small quantities. Such foods are concentrated, quickly satisfy a hunger, and require no refrigeration.

SPECIFIC PROBLEMS

Motion sickness. If your dog is subject to it, restrict food intake for twelve hours before a trip and water intake for one hour before travel time.

You can buy over-the-counter motion sickness pills, such as Dramamine, at any drugstore, after checking with your veterinarian for a recommendation.

Even with the pills, your dog may still get sick after being on the road awhile. The discomfort will be evidenced by drooling, panting, and pacing.

Pull over and stop.

The symptoms will clear up shortly. You can then repeat the medication and continue on your way, but try to restrict your dog's movements. Keeping the animal from roving about inside the car will decrease the chance of its getting sick all over again.

Hyperactivity. Some dogs can't—or won't—settle down in a car. If you happen to own one that makes you, and itself, a nervous wreck on the road, ask your veterinarian about tranquilizers.

Give the medication on an empty stomach one or two hours before departure.

You'll get where you're going feeling a lot better about the trip. And so will your dog.

9

BLESSED AND NOT SO BLESSED EVENTS

Happiness is, indeed, a warm puppy. One warm puppy. Dealing with expectant mothers, new mothers, and their multiple offspring is not for the average household pet owner.

Particularly when the household pet is a mixed breed and can only produce puppies of still greater mixed heritage. Puppies who, though warm, too often never find a home.

If you own a specific breed of dog and would like more of the same, see a professional breeder and your veterinarian, then follow their instructions to the letter.

Never attempt any form of "backyard" breeding.

If you don't own a purebred, it is strongly recommended here that you have the animal neutered. Male or female, they'll live healthier lives and become better pets, and you'll help reduce the population of unwanted animals.

Should the thought of neutering your female dog somehow offend you, you must resort to confinement and closely supervised outings during estrus. You may not want her breeding, but, remember, your neighbor's male dog doesn't care what you want.

However, dogs will be dogs.

Females in heat are mostly floozies. Males in the vicinity of such females are determined lechers.

If the two get together, don't try to separate them by force. You can seriously injure both. Besides, it's too late by then to do anything except let nature take its course and hope for the best. Currently, there are no abortion inducive medications available that are safe to use, in our opinion.

My God, she's pregnant!. Whether you say it in anguish or thanks, you now have sixty-three days, give or take three or four, until the main event.

Pregnancy will be evident by the third or fourth week when the breasts of your mother-to-be enlarge, and she begins to lose her girlish figure.

She may require increased protein and vitamin/mineral supplements in her diet. Exercise her routinely (obesity creates delivery problems), but exercise her with caution. The first three weeks are a very delicate time for fetuses. Use common sense. No Frisbees, please, and consult your veterinarian.

Planning a birthday. Long before a woman gives birth, she has a doctor and a safe place to have her baby. Or babies. Your dog should have the same.

If you don't create a place for her to have her puppies, she will create one herself—maybe in the middle of your bed. We recommend you build a box at least six inches wider and longer than the dog. The box should have an interior overhanging shelf all around, to serve as a barrier the puppies can get under to avoid being lain or rolled on.

The best bedding material to use is plain absorbent paper. Things are going to get a little messy in this maternity ward. Paper is easy to replace, and unlike straw or shavings, paper presents nothing for puppies to choke on.

Put the whelping box in a quiet area, indoors. Introduce your dog to it two or three weeks before she's due, to make sure she knows it's "her place."

Since more puppies are killed by chilling than by anything else, be prepared to provide a heat source that will maintain the area temperature at eighty-five to ninety degrees the first week and eighty to eighty-five degrees

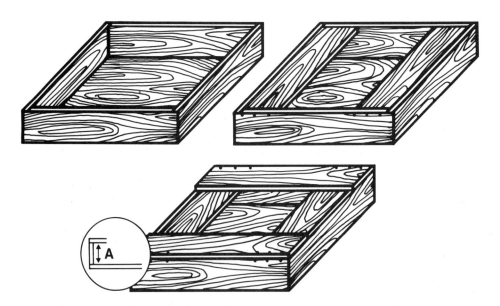

Whelping box. A whelping box can be made from almost any kind of lumber as long as the lumber is smooth and free of splinters. It's basically a child's sand box with seating on all four sides instead of just two. Note the cross-section insert. Make sure the height at "A" is less than the width of the mother's midsection. This will allow the puppies to escape being rolled on by crawling under the overhanging boards. Remember to place the heat source off to one side or the other and not directly over the box.

the second. A large, infrared heat lamp—placed off to one side, not beating directly down—is the best. Heating pads are the worst. They tend to dehydrate the newborns.

The birthday. Three or four days before The Day, your dog will begin nesting. She's thinking seriously about having a family. She'll lie down, think about it, get up, lie down again, and think some more.

When she decides she's ready, she'll lie down, stay down, and start straining to produce a puppy. Don't get nervous if she doesn't succeed right away, but if there are no results after an hour, it's time to call your veterinarian.

Don't be concerned if the puppy isn't born head first, either. With dogs, it doesn't matter which end greets the world. Also, an hour can pass between one head, or tail, being presented and the next.

If the new mom doesn't lick each puppy, breaking the umbilical cord in the process, stick your finger in the ignored newborn's mouth to remove the placenta and clear out the air passages. Then, tear off—*do not cut*—the cord about one inch from the body. Just pinch it between your fingers and pull sharply. Encourage the puppy to breathe by blowing in its mouth. Then give the pup to its mother.

The happy family. Your new mom is resting, the puppies are nursing nicely, and you're finding each and every one of them irresistible.

Don't touch them. Don't let anyone else touch them. Leave them completely alone for the first six to eight hours.

Doing otherwise can be upsetting to the mother. She might stop nursing and could actually kill her pups in her attempts to protect them.

After six to eight hours, whoever the dog trusts most can take her out for water and a walk while another member of your family cleans out the whelping box—being especially careful of the little ones left behind, of course—and replaces the bedding.

After twenty-four hours, a family visit to the veterinarian is imperative.

Quick weaning. When they're four to six weeks old, the puppies will be tearing up the place—and mom's breasts—with their little teeth and nails. You can trim the nails, but there's nothing you can do to dull the teeth. Allowing things to continue will only cause serious problems for the mother.

So, while she's out for a walk, wet down a puppy chow or a mixture of canned meat and cereal. Really goop it up. Turn it into a soup. The pups will walk in it, roll in it, but soon learn to eat it if you nurse them off your finger and push their faces into the bowl three or four times a day.

Meanwhile, keep their mother away from them for longer periods of time. Eventually, only bring her back at night.

When the puppies are eating well on their own, separate them from the mother completely. By the time they've reached seven weeks of age, they should be given up to their new homes before they become too attached to their present one.

The empty nest. The pups are gone, but mom's hormones are still at full steam, and her system won't adjust immediately to not having her family around. She may still look for them in the area previously occupied by the whelping box and even resort to carrying around dolls if she misses them too much.

You can help her through these post parting blues by reducing her fluids and perhaps administering a dose of milk of magnesia to dry up her milk.

SPECIFIC PROBLEMS

False pregnancy. Your female dog has been in heat, hasn't been bred, but thinks she has.

She'll start nesting and carrying a doll or rubber toy around, preparing for something that's not going to happen. The fantasy can make her fiercely protective of whatever she latches on to as a substitute puppy.

You may run out of tolerance and patience and even have to reduce her fluids to dry up her breasts, but she should get over it in five to seven days. If she doesn't, see your veterinarian.

Orphan puppies. Either mom died giving birth or has decided motherhood is not for her. Either way, if they are to live, her puppies will have to be fed and otherwise cared for.

Room temperature: Ninety degrees for the first week in a dry area. A cold vaporizer, available at your local pharmacy, should be operated in the room and away from the puppies.

Feeding formula: Half a cup of homogenized milk fortified with the yolk of an egg and a tablespoon of white corn syrup in a nursing bottle will substitute in an emergency for mother's milk. However, over the long haul, a commercial formula available in a pet store is much preferred.

Feeding method: Use a preemie bottle, doll nursing bottle, or puppy nursing bottle—the latter being available at any good pet supply store. Feed each puppy four or five times a day. Don't overfeed. When the tummy has become extended a little, he or she has had enough.

After feeding: Gently caress each pup and wipe it with a warm, wet cloth to encourage burping and elimination. To keep their skins moist, apply a cream or lotion containing aloe.

Caution: Between feedings, your orphans might pick up the habit of suckling on one another's feet or tails. If they do, separate them. The habit is a harmful one and could bring about infections and digestive problems.

10 "MY DOG WAS JUST HIT BY A CAR!"

Someday, there may be an ambulance service for small animals, complete with paramedics, as there is for people. Until then, if your dog is struck by a moving vehicle, the only one on the scene to help may be you.

It's not going to be easy.

You'll naturally be very upset. Cars do serious damage to living beings of any size.

This chapter concerns itself with what you can do, and what you should not do, right after the accident.

The procedures that follow are not necessarily to be performed in the order given. What you do and don't do depends on the injury. So read the whole chapter, then reread it as many times as necessary to understand how to act quickly and correctly in any given circumstances.

IN GENERAL

1. Call your veterinarian. *Then stay off the phone.* Most veterinarians are required to provide emergency service—no matter what time of day or night the accident happens. If you get an answering service when you make the call, don't grab the yellow pages and start working your way down the list. If your line is busy, there's no way your doctor or the doctor on call for emergencies can reach you.

2. Don't create another emergency by getting yourself hit. Have someone—a friend, a bystander, *anyone*—take charge of traffic and direct it around the scene of the accident. In other words, do the same for your dog as you would for a person. This will prevent further injury to the animal—and injury to you.

3. Is your dog conscious? The only time a dog closes its eyes is when it's

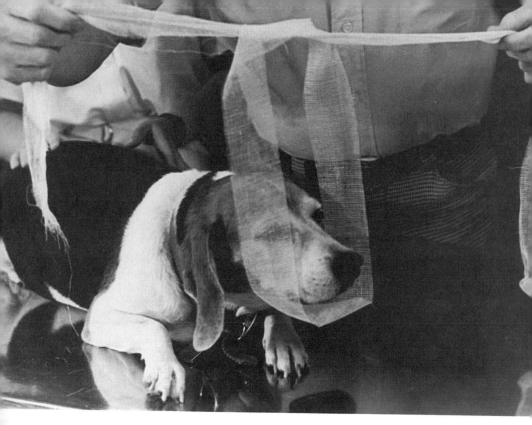

Securing jaws with gauze bandage. Make a loop using a simple overhand knot. Place the loop over the jaws and tighten the knot sufficiently to hold the jaws together. Wrap around the muzzle two or three times. Cross under the jaw. Tie off behind the ears.

alseep. Unless your dog is obviously alert, take time to observe it. Does it react to your voice? Does it focus on you? If the accident has happened at night, flash a light in your dog's eyes to see if its pupils react.

4. If your dog is conscious, *Don't touch it.* You'll want to touch it in an attempt to comfort it. But remember, the animal has, to its way of thinking, been attacked. Your touch of tenderness can be, and often is, misunderstood as a continuation of that attack. Being in pain and dazed, your dog may bite you if it can. It has happened between the very best of friends.

5. Before you touch a conscious animal, secure its jaws. *Do not use a cheap, over-the-counter muzzle.* Such netlike muzzles have a serious flaw—they allow the animal to bite, but don't allow the jaws to open wide enough to release its hold. There is a better, gentler way—easier on the animal and certainly easier on you. Here, a roll of gauze bandage is used to demonstrate the technique.

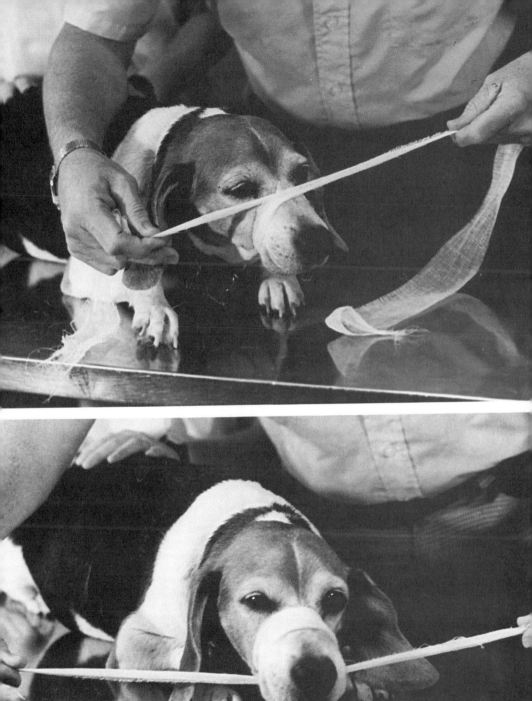

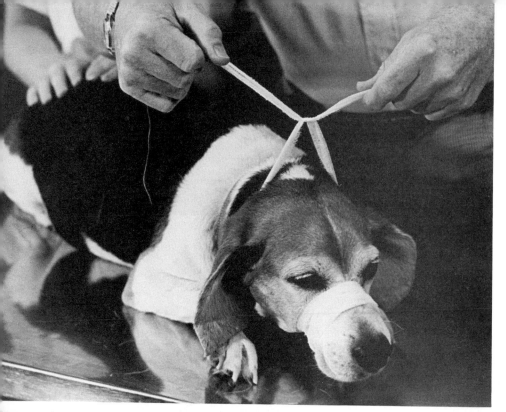

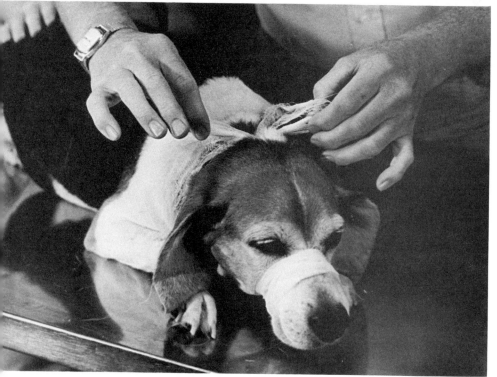

If you don't have a roll of gauze bandage, tear a T-shirt or any piece of cloth into strips as a substitute. Lacking all of the above, you may use a leash, a piece of rope, a belt, or a pair of stockings as shown.

Securing jaws with belt or leash. Loop the end of the leash, or the loop you make from rope, belt, or stockings, over the neck. Wrap the muzzle, bring the free end under the jaws, and hold in place behind the head by grasping collar and free end in one hand.

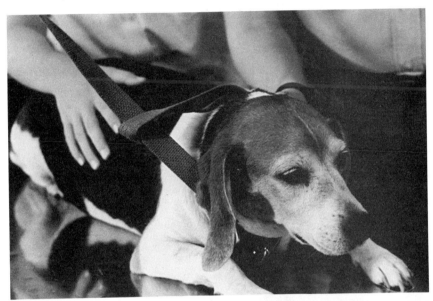

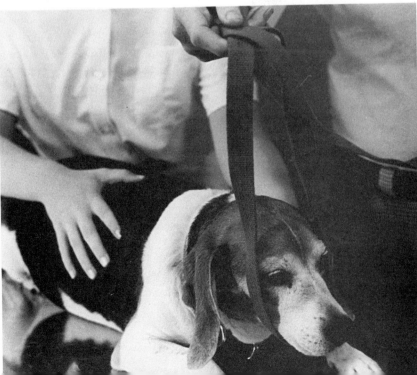

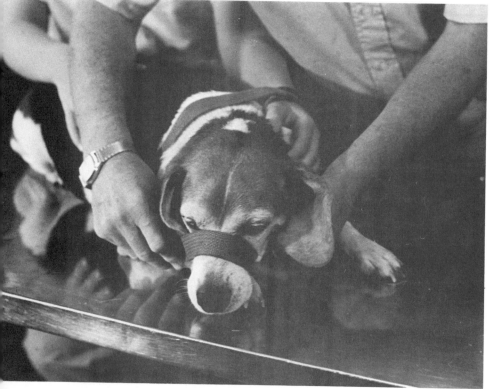

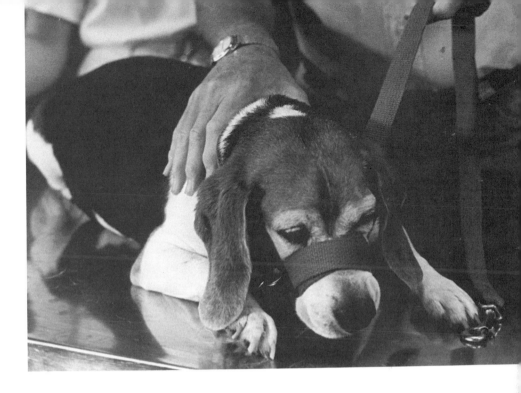

Bite protection for pug, Pekinese, and bulldog. With some dogs you won't be able to secure the jaws as previously shown. Instead, loosely wrap a towel around the dog's neck and hold it there. The towel's bulk will prevent the animal from reaching you with its teeth.

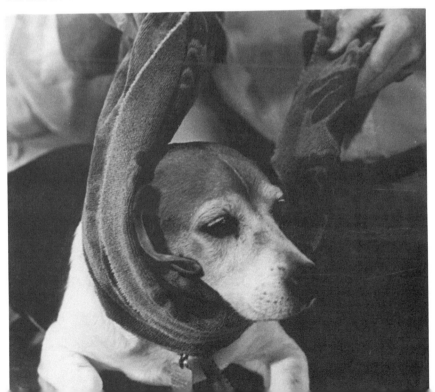

6. If your dog is unconscious. If it doesn't respond to normal stimuli, don't follow your instinct to grab it in your arms and pick it up. There may be internal injuries or bone damage that you'd only make worse by doing so.

7. Move your dog off the road. Conscious or unconscious, *get the dog to the side of the road.* It's even more important to do so at night, when another vehicle could come along and compound the damage already done.

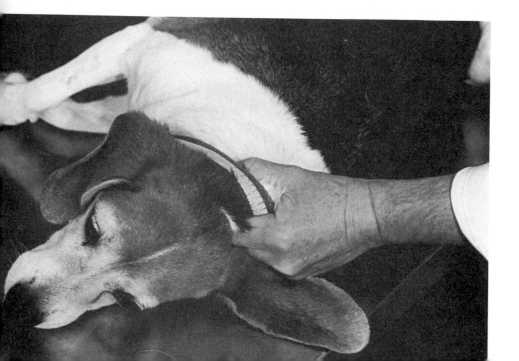

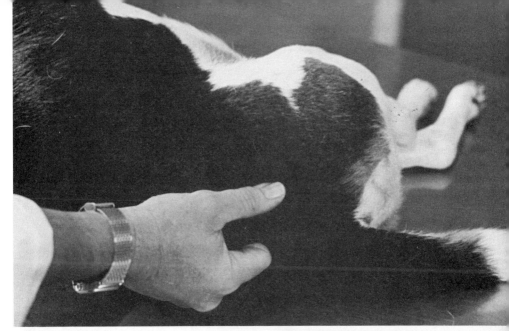

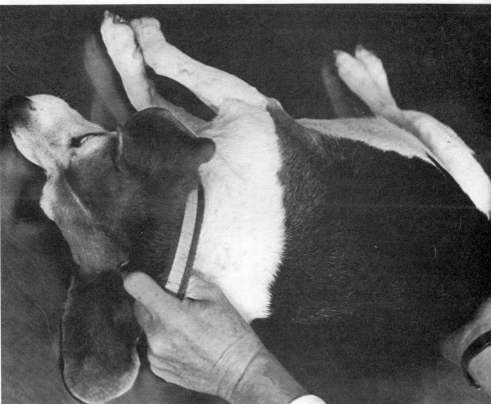

Moving dog off road. Grasp the animal by the loose flesh at the back of its neck. At the same time, secure a similar hold on the animal's hindquarters. Do not lift. *Slide* the animal along the ground until you have reached the side of the road.

8. Making a stretcher and using it. You probably won't have time to make one when the accident has just happened, so have it ready ahead of time. A piece of plywood large enough to carry the animal and thick enough to support its weight firmly serves the purpose.

Using a stretcher. Put a blanket under the stretcher. Do not lift the animal onto the stretcher. *Slide* it on, using the same two-hand hold used for sliding it off the road. To keep your dog as quiet as possible during transport to the veterinarian, wrap the blanket around it and the stretcher.

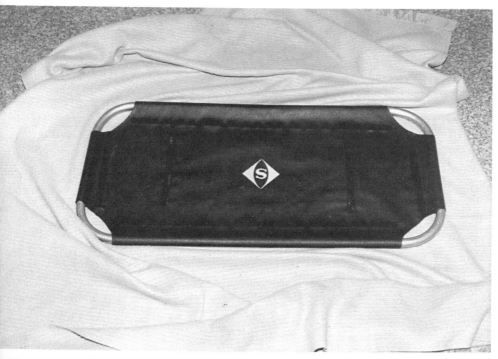

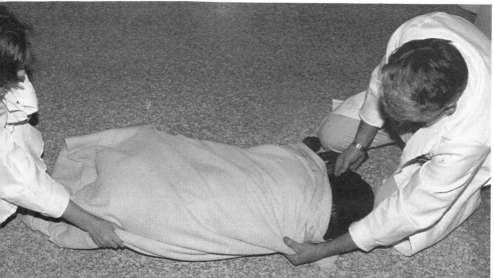

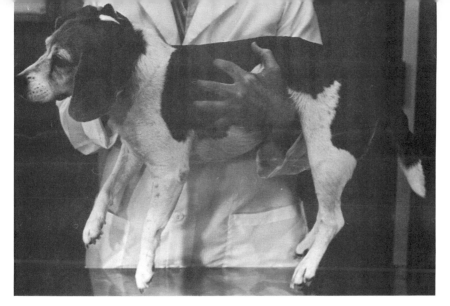

Lifting a small dog. Grasp skin and collar, if there is a collar, alongside the dog's head with one hand. Place the other under its stomach about midway between forelegs and hind legs. Lift with both arms, keeping the animal as level as possible.

9. How to pick up an injured dog. Lacking a stretcher and the time to make one on the spot, you'll have no choice but to lift up your dog in your arms. If you do it as follows, you'll cause the smallest amount of secondary damage.

Lifting a large dog. Grasp skin and collar, if there is one, alongside the head with one hand. Place the other under the chest just to the rear of the forelegs. Have whoever is helping you place one hand under the dog's stomach and the other just forward of the hind legs. Lift in unison to keep the animal level.

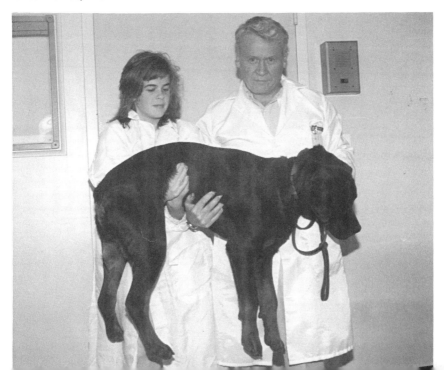

10. Taking your dog to the doctor. Unless the following section, Specific Injuries, indicates differently, keep your dog lying flat and take it easy getting to the veterinarian. Bouncing an injured animal around can only make things worse.

Do not feed or water the dog. Do not make getting to the doctor a family project. Leave as many as possible at home. Do not forget to call ahead or have someone else call ahead and tell the doctor you're on your way.

If the veterinarian on call isn't your regular veterinarian, be prepared to tell him or her your dog's medical history and when it had its last meal.

Finally, once the animal is in the doctor's care, *please* make yourself scarce.

SPECIFIC INJURIES

Broken leg. Don't try to straighten it out. Don't use a splint. Gently place the limb in a relatively normal position, move your dog off the road, immobilize the limb, and transport the animal to the doctor.

Compound fracture. The difference between a compound and a simple fracture is easily seen. With a compound fracture, the bone has broken through the skin, and there is likely to be severe bleeding. Place a gauze pad or folded cloth over the bleeding and immobilize the leg with a towel as shown previously for a simple fracture.

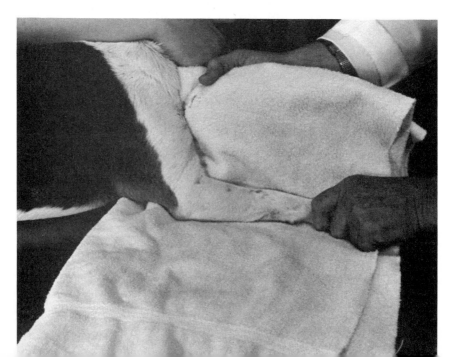

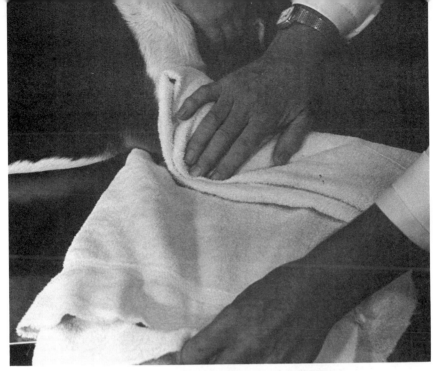

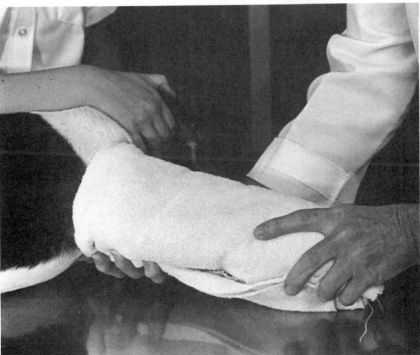

Broken leg. Depending on the size of the dog, and the leg, use a small, medium, or large towel. Carefully wrap the towel around the leg as many times as possible. The towel's bulk will restrict, if not totally prevent, the animal from moving the limb and aggravating the injury.

Large laceration, little bleeding. It's amazing how large a wound can be and bleed so little. Do not apply iodine, methiolate, peroxide, or other household first aid liquids that you might use on your own cuts and scrapes. If you use *plain* petroleum jelly, a first aid cream, or lotion, they will keep the wound from drying out and protect it until it can be professionally treated.

Bleeding paw. An injured paw will often bleed profusely. Press a gauze pad or clean, folded cloth directly over the wound. Bandage as shown to maintain pressure during transport.

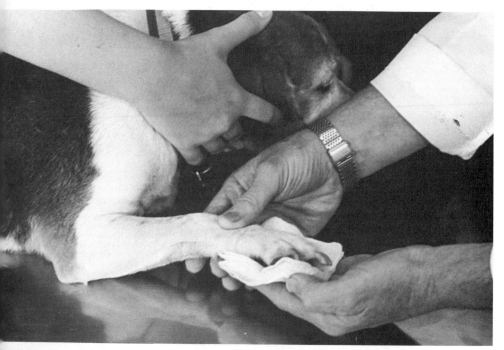

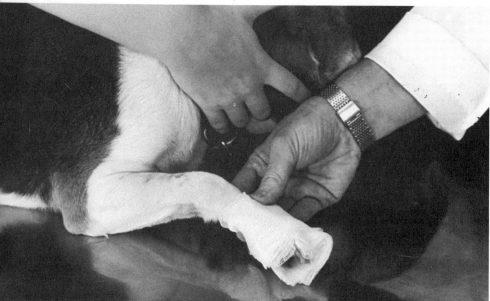

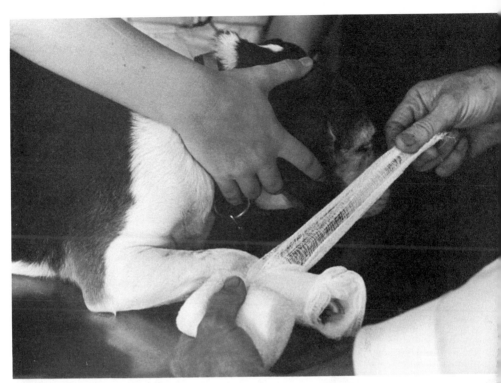

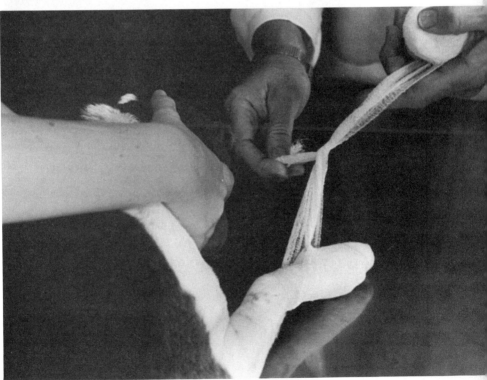

Heavily bleeding wound. Such wounds indicate that a major blood vessel has been severed. Do not apply the traditional tourniquet. Unless the animal is bleeding from the nose or mouth, put pressure over the area the bleeding is coming from and bandage.

Bleeding side. An injury to the side is treated similarly to a paw injury. Place the pad over the wound. Apply pressure and maintain it with two or three wraps of gauze or strips of cloth. Be careful. Don't wrap the bandage so tight it restricts breathing.

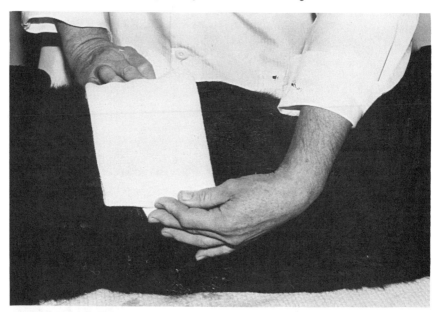

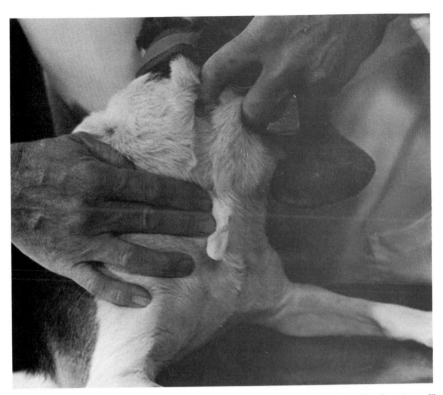

Throat wound. If the wound is in a area that cannot be bandaged, such as the throat, you'll have to maintain pressure against the wound by holding a clean pad in place against it.

Eye injury. A small dog is more often the victim of an eye injury than a large one. The force of impact can cause one or both eyes, partially or totally to pop out of their sockets. If the damage is partial, the eye can be saved. In the extreme injury, saving the sight of the animal is very doubtful. However, the following first aid measures should be taken in either case.

Do not touch the eye. Wet a soft, light cloth with clean water. A piece of T-shirt will do. Gently cover the injury and keep the dressing moist on the trip to the veterinarian.

Bleeding from mouth or nose. Do not muzzle the dog. This is one of the times to break that rule. Oral or nasal bleeding is generally caused by a broken jaw, loosened teeth, a fractured skull, or because the animal has bitten through its tongue. *Muzzling or securing the jaws may cause choking.* However, unless the dog is unconscious, you must still protect yourself from being bitten. With a small dog, it's not difficult to do. With a large one, you'll need help. Probably a lot of help.

Restraint in cases of oral or nasal bleeding. You'll need two belts, two leashes, or two pieces of rope. Depending on the size of the dog, you'll need one or two extra people. Loop one restraining line over the dog's head and maintain light tension on it to one side. Loop over the second restraining line and maintain tension on it to the opposite side. By keeping careful control of both lines, you can manage, without choking the animal, to prevent it from turning its head around to reach any of you with its teeth.

If it is a large dog—and there's no help in sight—you'll have no choice but to muzzle the animal. Use a single leash to do it as previously shown. As soon as the dog is in the car, *take the muzzle off.*

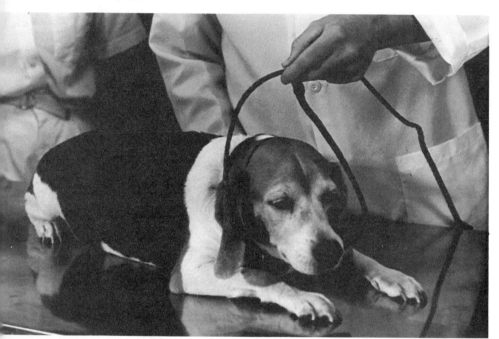

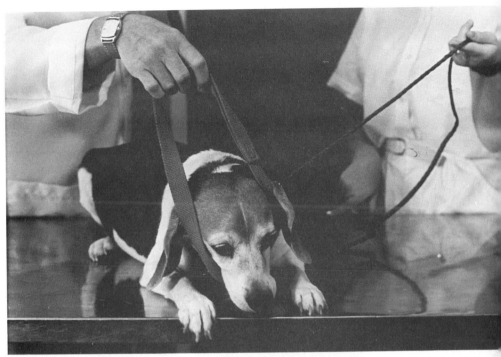

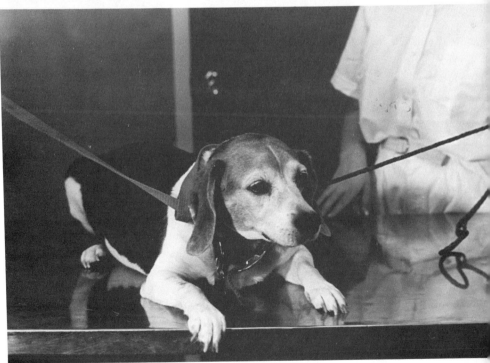

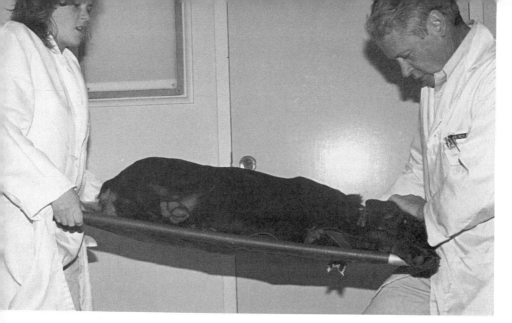

Transport position, oral or nasal bleeding. To keep the dog from choking on the way to the doctor due to the bleeding itself, maintain it in a position that keeps its head lower than its body. Though not shown here, the restraint lines should be employed during the entire trip.

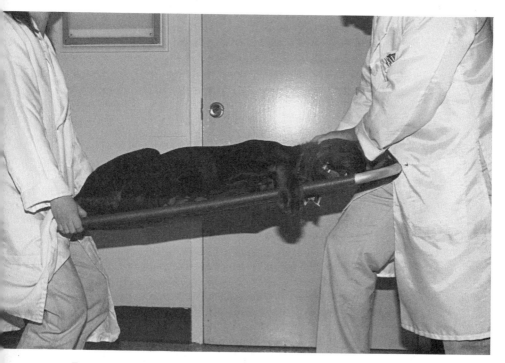

Transport, internal bleeding. During transport, maintain the animal in a position that keeps its head higher than its body. This prevents the dog's choking as a result of the internal hemorrhaging.

Internal bleeding. When the animal is coughing up bloody foam, that is an indication of hemorrhaging into the lungs or upper respiratory system. *You can't stop the bleeding, and this is another time you can't secure the animal's jaws.* Protect yourself from being bitten as shown in the section on bleeding from the mouth or nose, on pages 78–79, and prepare the dog for transport.

Shock. Basically, if an animal is unconscious, consider it to be in shock. Shallow breathing is one indication. Another is condition of the inner surface of the lips: pale and cold.

Shock is not a problem first aid can do much to relieve. You can help, though, by not letting your pet become further chilled and by keeping its air passages open. In your attempt to keep the dog from becoming cold, don't bundle it up to the point where it will become overheated. Never give it anything to drink. Keep its mouth open and its tongue out during transport.

Severe loss of skin, tissue, and muscle. This is a very common injury, and most dog owners are more than surprised at how well it heals. What you must do is, once again, keep the injured area from drying out before it receives medical attention.

Severe skin loss. Wet down a T-shirt or towel with clean water. Entirely cover the wound with it. Keep the dressing moist during transport.

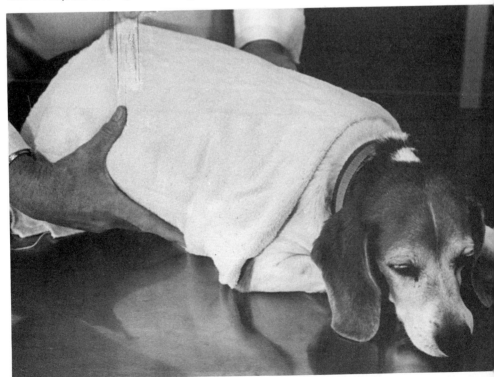

Evisceration. The shock of seeing your dog's internal organs out of their abdominal cavity is one you must overcome if you're going to help. Just remember, if your pet is to have a chance to live, you *must* help—and you'll need assistance.

Evisceration. Do not attempt to wash or apply antiseptic to the exposed organs. Lift the animal and its organs simultaneously. Place both on a wet towel, the size of the towel depending on the size of the dog. Wrap animal and organs securely in the towel and keep the towel moist during the trip to the veterinarian.

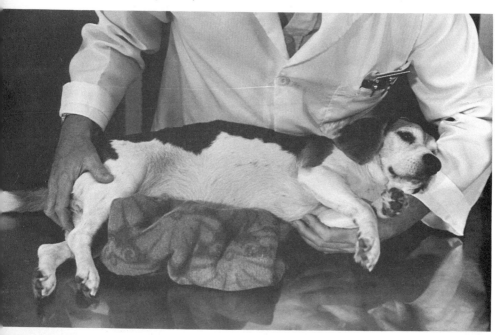

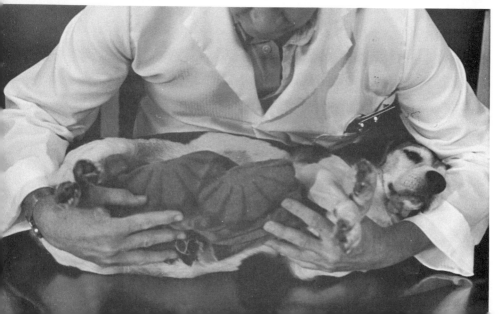

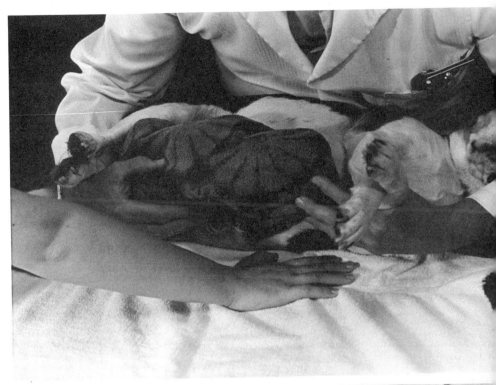

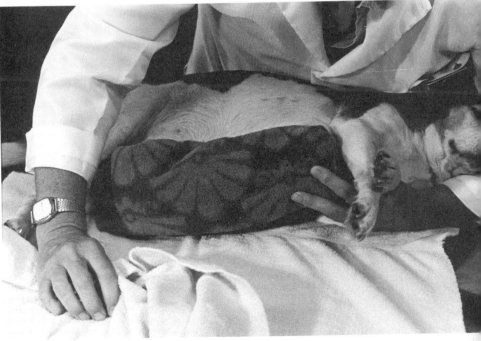

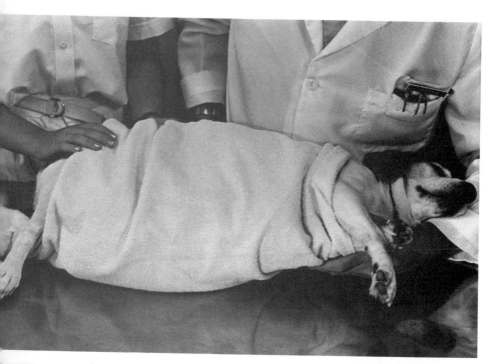

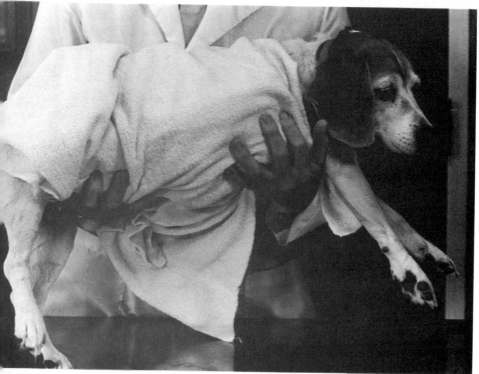

11

COMMON HOUSEHOLD POISONS AND POISONOUS PLANTS

Most, if not all, harmful household products come in "child-proof" containers. You know, the kind with caps and closures adults have trouble opening?

However, a child-proof container isn't dog-proof. Dogs are able to chew, climb, jump, and dig better than small children, and they're just as eager to explore. Closing up, capping up, and locking up such containers will prevent any emergency caused by ingestion of or exposure to their contents.

POISONOUS HOME PRODUCTS

The accompanying chart lists several poisonous or potentially poisonous products.

Inducing vomiting. In most cases, initial treatment requires you to make your dog throw up. How to do so was shown previously in Chapter 4, pages 37–39, but the instant replay below will save you much flipping of pages.

1. Force the dog to swallow three to four teaspoons of hydrogen peroxide.
2. Force the dog to swallow a strong salt-water solution. 3. Stick your finger down the dog's throat.

POISONOUS PLANTS

Many household plants, even common shrubs, can be toxic to the ever-curious dog. This is especially true of younger pups, whose dogma dictates: If it doesn't move fast enough, eat it!

Listed below are several flora that may be toxic to your dog and the suggested first aid measures to be taken in case of ingestion. Most are not fatal, but they can certainly be upsetting to your dog—and therefore to you.

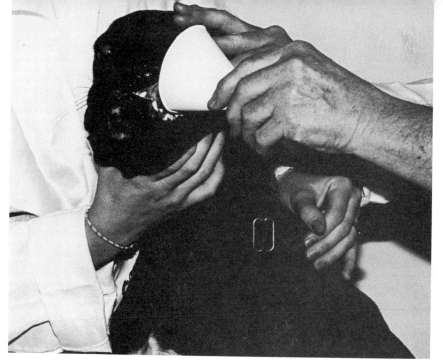

Inducing vomiting by forced swallowing. Hold open the large pocket at the rear of your dog's mouth with one hand and pour in the solutions of peroxide or salt with the other. You may or may not need assistance to hold the animal's head still.

Administering dosages. To administer liquid, hold the pocket between your dog's lips and jaw open and pour in the recommended amount. To administer a pill or two, grasp them between your two fingers, force or cajole the jaws open, slide the two fingers well back in the mouth and deposit the medication over the curvature of the tongue. Then, gently stroke the dog's throat while as gently holding its jaws closed (after removing your fingers, of course).

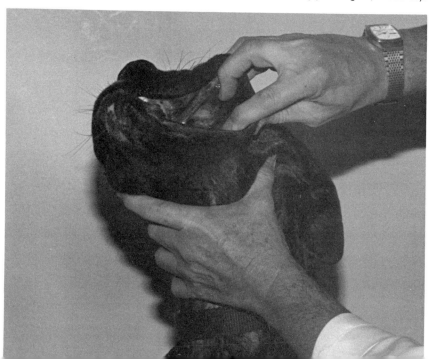

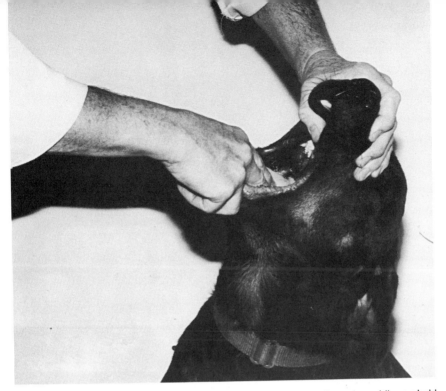

Inducing vomiting with fingers. Use two fingers to force open the lower jaw while you hold the upper jaw near the nose with the other hand. Push your fingers over the tongue and far enough down the dog's throat to induce gagging. We stress caution with your grip on the upper jaw. Pinching your dog's lips against its teeth could cause it to clamp down on the fingers in its mouth.

The list is by no means all-inclusive, so should your pet make a meal of a plant not listed, call your veterinarian.

Group One. Apple, almond, apricot, cherry, hydrangea, peach.

This group can produce symptoms related to cyanide poisoning if consumed in sufficient amounts, which is rare in dogs. If such consumption is observed, *induce vomiting*. Signs of poisoning are difficulty in breathing, bright red mouth membranes, and collapse. If they develop, call your veterinarian.

Group two. Amaryllis, azalea, bird of paradise plant, daffodil, holly, honeysuckle, hyacinth, mushrooms, privet, rhododendron, yew (Taxus).

Usually not serious, but induce vomiting, and administer a stomach-coating agent. If vomiting and diarrhea continue, call your veterinarian.

Group three. Bleeding heart.

Can be serious if enough is consumed. Induce vomiting immediately. Convulsions may occur. Call your veterinarian.

Product	How Serious	First Aid	Signs of Poisoning	Second Treatment
Alcohol, beer	Moderate	Induce vomiting.	Staggering, coma	See a veterinarian
Antifreeze, deicers	Very	Induce vomiting, call vet.	Staggering, vomiting, blindness	See a vet.
Aspirin-related drugs	Moderate to very	Induce vomiting, call vet.	Depression, weakness, vomiting	See a vet.
Bleach	Moderate to very	*Do not cause vomiting.* Give milk of magnesia. Flush skin/eyes with water.	Burned skin, difficulty breathing, vomiting	See a vet.
Chocolate, caffeine	Not serious to very, depending on amount	Induce vomiting.	Hyperactity, vomiting	See a vet.
Detergents, Ammonia	Very	*Do not cause vomiting,* give milk or milk of magnesia. Flush skin with water.	Depression, continual vomiting, coma	See a vet.
Dish/laundry detergents, shampoo	Moderate	Flush with water; give mild vinegar solution.	Skin irritation, vomiting, diarrhea	Pepto-Bismol or similar stomach coating agent.
Drain cleaners	Very (caustic)	*Do not cause vomiting.* Flush with water or mild vinegar solution; give mild vinegar or milk; see a vet.	Skin irritation, oral burns, difficulty swallowing	See a vet.
Fertilizers	Usually not serious	Give Kaopectate or similar emulsion.	Vomiting, diarrhea	See a vet.

Product	How Serious	First Aid	Signs of Poisoning	Second Treatment
Fuels, volatile cleaners, solvents	Moderate to very	If ingested, *do not cause vomiting.* See a vet.	Difficulty breathing	See a vet.
		Skin contact: Flush with water, apply mineral oil to area, bathe.	Burns	See a vet.
Insecticide	Not serious to very	Depends on active agent. Call vet.	Variable	See a vet.
Matches	Moderate	Induce vomiting, then give stomach-coating emulsion.	Continual vomiting, difficulty breathing	See a vet.
Perfumes	Very	If ingested: induce vomiting, then give Digel or similar.	Difficulty breathing, hyperactivity, coma.	See a vet.
		Skin contact: flush area with mineral oil, apply cortisone ointment.	Burns	See a vet.
Marijuana	Not serious to moderate	Induce vomiting. No sedatives, no aspirin.	Hyperactivity, vomiting, depression	See a vet.
Rodenticides, D-Con, strychnine	Moderate to very	Induce vomiting. Call a vet.	Hemorrhage, convulsions	See a vet.
Snow/ice salts	Not serious	Flush area, apply mineral oil, cortisone ointment.	Burns	See a vet.
		Ingested: rare. Flush with water. Give stomach-coating emulsion.		
Weed killer	Very	See a vet.		

Group four. Elephant ear, philodendron.

Very irritating to throat and mouth. Therefore, flush mouth with cold water after inducing vomiting. A stomach-coating agent may be administered, but there is danger of kidney failure, so call your veterinarian.

Group five. Lily of the valley.

Can have a direct effect on the heart. Induce vomiting, and call your veterinarian.

Group six. Marijuana, morning glory.

Can alter behavior, causing depression or hyperactivity. Induce vomiting, and call your veterinarian.

Group seven. Eggplant, jasmine, nightshade, potato.

Induce vomiting and administer a stomach-coating agent. Continued vomiting, pain, and diarrhea can precede collapse, so call your veterinarian.

Group eight. Nettle.

Nettle actually injects a substance into the animal's membranes, so flush the mouth thoroughly with water.

The substance can cause vomiting, cardiac problems, and collapse that require immediate veterinary care.

Group nine. Mistletoe, poinsettia.

Can cause cardiac problems and collapse. Induce vomiting, and call your veterinarian.

Group ten. Pyracantha.

These plants are not poisonous as such, but their thorns can cause the same problems as foreign bodies—including abscesses. Therefore, remove any visible thorns and be alert for infections. If they occur, consult your veterinarian.

Group eleven. Tobacco.

May cause excessive salivation, vomiting, and collapse. Call your veterinarian.

12 SUGGESTED DRUG DOSAGES

Since dogs come in all sizes, it's difficult to offer a single dosage formula. The right dose for a large dog would be an overdose for a small dog. It's a good idea to know—or at least have a pretty good idea of—your dog's weight. When in doubt, give a lesser dose than the one indicated or consult your veterinarian.

In the list below, "60 pounds" (or whatever number) indicates the general area of your pet's weight.

Aspirin (buffered of otherwise). Use for pain, arthritic problems. Very mild sedative action. Caution: It can be toxic to very small dogs.

1 adult tablet—60 pounds—every 6 to 8 hours.

1 "baby" tablet—15 pounds—every 6 to 8 hours.

¼ "baby" tablet if under 15 pounds—every 6 to 8 hours.

Charcoal. Absorbs toxic material, also helps reduce flatulence. Available in powder or tablets. Follow directions on container.

Cold medicines. Liquids containing decongestant such as Pseudophed and cough depressants such as Guaifenensin

Up to 30 pounds: ½ to 1 tablespoon every 4 hours

Over 30 pounds: 1 tablespoon to 2 tablespoons every 4 hours

Cold allergy tablets containing antihistamine such as Chlorophenisamine

Up to 30 pounds: 1 child's tablet, 2 to 3 times a day

Over 30 pounds: 1 adult tablet, 2 to 3 times a day

Note: Your veterinarian or pharmacist can advise you which over-the-counter remedies contain the above medications.

Cough medicines. (nonprescription):

Up to 30 pounds, administer child's dose.

Over 30 pounds, administer 12-years-and-older dose.

Antiacid/antigas emulsions.
1 teaspoon for every 5 pounds—as often as needed. Cannot overdose.

Dramamine.
To prevent motion sickness. Best administered on an empty stomach 1 to 2 hours before travel.
Up to 30 pounds, child dose.
Over 30 pounds, adult dose.

Hydrogen peroxide (medicinal).
Wounds: Apply full strength, then flush thoroughly with water.
To induce vomiting: Force down 3 to 4 teaspoons orally every few minutes until vomiting occurs.

Kaopectate (or similar emulsion).
Soothes stomach/intestines. Use for vomiting, diarrhea, certain poisons.
1 teaspoon for small dogs.
2 to 3 tablespoons for large dogs.
Administer every 2 to 3 hours. If the problem persists after 12 hours, call a veterinarian.

Milk of magnesia.
Used as an antacid, antitoxin, and laxative.
1 tablespoon for every 30 pounds. Repeat in 12 hours. If the problem persists, call a veterinarian.

Mineral oil.
Apply to hair to soften paints, absorb solvents and petroleum products, then wash with mild detergent.

Pepto-Bismol (or similar stomach-coating agent).
Very effective against simple vomiting and diarrhea. Can be administered frequently.
1 teaspoon for every 20 pounds as needed.

Sodium bicarbonate (powdered).
Use to neutralize acid.
1 teaspoon in 8 ounces of water. Administer 1 to 4 teaspoons of this solution as needed for mild upset stomach.
3 teaspoons in 8 ounces of water. For acid burns, use this solution to flush skin area thoroughly.

Vinegar.
Use to neutralize alkalines, such as lye.
Orally: 1 teaspoon in 8 ounces of water. Administer freely.
Skin: Flush area freely with undiluted vinegar.

MEDICAL
RECORDS

MEDICAL RECORD

Name _____

Date of Birth _____

Breed _____ Sex _____

Owner _____

Address _____

_____

City _____ State _____ Zip _____

Acquired from: _____

_____

SURGICAL HISTORY

Age	Date	Veterinarian	Proceedure

EXAMINATIONS

Age	Date	Physical	External Parasites	Fecal	Heartworm	Canine Brucellosis

VACCINATIONS

Age	Date	Rabies	Distemper, Hepatitis, Parainfluenza	Leptospirosis	Parvovirus	Carona Virus

PARASITE TREATMENTS

Age	Date	Heartworms	Roundworms	Hookworms	Tapeworms	Whipworms

INDEX

Abscesses, 12, 13, 41, 90
Accidents
    dog struck by car, 61–82
Airways, open, 12, 32
Allergic reactions, 24
Allergies
    from flea bites, 50–51
    skin, 13–14
Aloe, 9
Anal glands (sacs), 41
Antiacid tablets, 41
Antiacid/antigas emulsions
    dosage, 91
Antibiotics, 3, 9
Antihistamine, 14, 24, 25
Artificial respiration, 32
Aspirin, 7, 43
    dosage, 91
Auto travel, 53–54
Automobiles
    dog struck by, 61–82

Baking soda, 12, 14
B–B shot, 13
Birthing, 56–57
Bite protection, 62, 67, 77, 81
Bites, animal, 12
Bladder problems, 44
Bleeding, 74
    ear wounds, 26
    heavy, 72, 76
    with injuries, 7, 13
    internal, 81
    from nose and mouth, 28, 29, 77
    from paw, 75
    pressure in control of, 13, 75, 76, 76
    from side, 76
    with skin injuries, 3–6
    restraint with, 78

transport positions with, 80
Bloat, 41
Blood tests, 50
Bones, 28–29
Breathing, 14
Breeding, 55
Broken leg, 72, 73
Brushing, 1
Bulldog, 67
Burns
    electric, 10–12
    forcing fluids with severe, 13
    minor, 9, 10
    severe, 12
    turpentine, 9–10

Cardiac problems, 90
    see also Heart failure
Cat bites, 12
Charcoal, 91
Checkups, annual, 18, 31, 50
Chemical burns, 9
Chewing (symptom), 1
Chicken soup, 40
Coat
    caring for, 1–3
Cold medicine, 28
    dosage, 91
Collapse, 90
Constipation, 41
Cortisone ointment, 9, 24, 25, 28
Cough, coughing, 31, 50
    bloody foam, 81
Cough medicines, 91
CPR, 33
Creams, ointments
    for skin problems, 1
    see also Cortisone ointment; First aid cream